THE
CASE FOR
GHOSTS

About the Author

A native of Minnesota but a resident of Colorado since 1969, Jeff's life has been a journey that has taken him down many different paths. Besides writing, his hobbies include reading, art, politics and political history, world and military history, religion and spirituality, numismatics (coin collecting), paleontology, astronomy (and science in general), and Fortean subjects such as Bigfoot, UFOs, and things that go bump in the night. His personal philosophy is that life is about learning and growing, both intellectually and spiritually, and that is the perspective from which he approaches each project he undertakes. Currently Jeff resides in Lakewood, CO, with his wife, Carol, and their two sons.

To Write to the Author

If you wish to contact the author or would like more information about this book, please write to the author in care of Llewellyn Worldwide and we will forward your request. Both the author and publisher appreciate hearing from you and learning of your enjoyment of this book and how it has helped you. Llewellyn Worldwide cannot guarantee that every letter written to the author can be answered, but all will be forwarded. Please write to:

J. Allan Danelek
℅ Llewellyn Worldwide
2143 Wooddale Drive, Dept. 0-7387-0865-8
Woodbury, Minnesota 55125-2989, U.S.A.

Please enclose a self-addressed stamped envelope for reply,
or $1.00 to cover costs. If outside U.S.A.,
enclose international postal reply coupon.

Many of Llewellyn's authors have websites with additional information and resources. For more information, please visit our website at www.llewellyn.com.

THE
CASE FOR
GHOSTS

AN OBJECTIVE LOOK AT THE PARANORMAL

J. ALLAN DANELEK

Llewellyn Publications
Woodbury, Minnesota

First Edition
First Printing, 2006

Book design by Steffani Chambers
Cover design by Gavin Dayton Duffy
Editing by Jane Hilken
Interior photographs property of author
Llewellyn is a registered trademark of Llewellyn Worldwide, Ltd.

Library of Congress Cataloging-in-Publication Data
Danelek, J. Allan, 1958-
   The case for ghosts : an objective look at the paranormal / J. Allan Danelek.
      p. cm.
   Includes bibliographical references and index.
   ISBN-13: 978-0-7387-0865-2
   ISBN-10: 0-7387-0865-8
   1. Ghosts. I. Title.

BF1461.D375 2006
133.1—dc22   2006040983

Llewellyn Worldwide does not participate in, endorse, or have any authority or responsibility concerning private business transactions between our authors and the public.
   All mail addressed to the author is forwarded but the publisher cannot, unless specifically instructed by the author, give out an address or phone number.
   Any Internet references contained in this work are current at publication time, but the publisher cannot guarantee that a specific location will continue to be maintained. Please refer to the publisher's website for links to authors' websites and other sources.

Llewellyn Publications
A Division of Llewellyn Worldwide, Ltd.
2143 Wooddale Drive, Dept. 0-7387-0856-8
Woodbury, Minnesota 55125-2989, U.S.A.
www.llewellyn.com

Printed in the United States of America

Other Books by J. Allan Danelek

Mystery of Reincarnation

Contents

Acknowledgments

I would like to thank Mr. Bryan Bonner at the Rocky Mountain Paranormal Society for his encouragement and assistance in going through this material and pointing out its many potential problems, possible pitfalls, and occasional bouts of just plain nonsense. Such oversights have since been corrected or otherwise taken into account, thus making this a better book than it would have been otherwise. If ghosts are ever to be proven to be a fact, it will be through the tireless efforts of dedicated and clever skeptics like himself, who have made it their life's passion to keep both believers and debunkers alike on their collective toes.

I also would like to thank my editor and all the staff at Llewellyn Publishing for their encouragement and ongoing enthusiasm for my work. It is impossible to speak to the human condition without the proper stage, and Llewellyn and the handful of publishers out there courageous enough to let people like myself take that stage are a true godsend.

Finally, I would be remiss if I didn't thank my wife Carol for her constant encouragement and loving support in all my writing projects, for I doubt if I could achieve much of anything without her. It just goes to prove the old adage that if one were to scratch a writer worth his or her salt, one will invariably find a supportive life partner and soul mate lying just beneath the surface. Thanks to all.

J. Allan Danelek
October, 2005

Introduction

Marley's Ghost: "You don't believe in me."

Scrooge: "I don't."

Marley's Ghost: "What evidence would you have of my reality beyond that of your senses?"

Scrooge: "I don't know."

Marley's Ghost: "Why do you doubt your senses?"

Scrooge: "Because a little thing affects them. A slight disorder of the stomach makes them cheats. You may be an undigested bit of beef, a blot of mustard, a crumb of cheese, a fragment of an underdone potato. There's more of gravy than of grave about you, whatever you are!"

—Charles Dickens, *A Christmas Carol*

Do you believe in ghosts? According to a Harris poll conducted in January, 2003, over half of the adult population of the United States, including nearly sixty-five percent of adults under the age of twenty-seven, do. Clearly, the belief that the human soul not only survives death but is capable of manifesting itself to the still-living not only has held steady for decades, but even seems to be on the upswing.

But why should this be? Why should otherwise level-headed men and women come to imagine there exists something that is neither visible to the naked eye nor discernible to our other senses, yet is as real and solid as any material object? Is the belief in ghosts nothing more than culturally influenced superstition that serves only to reflect our fears about our own mortality, or could there be something more to it?

No doubt ghosts do reflect some of our concerns about what happens to us after we die. After all, if there are ghosts, then it demonstrates that the human personality does survive death, giving all of us the hope of immortality. As such, even while they frequently terrify us, it seems we need ghosts, if only for our own personal sense of cosmic significance.

But if the belief in ghosts were nothing more than a byproduct of mankind's fear of death and its ongoing quest for immortality, it would be easy to dismiss the entire subject as so much superstitious nonsense and move on, but even in our supposedly scientific age the subject continues to hold sway over us. It seems we simply cannot shake the notion that the belief in ghosts has more to say to us than that we live on after death.

Ghosts appear to be something we believe not so much on a rational, empirical level, but on an intuitive or even emotional level. Like the belief in God, they are something we "feel" to be true even though few of us have ever had a genuine paranormal experience. They speak to us of the mysteries of the universe and reinforce our inherent beliefs that there is much more to the cosmos than what tiny bit we can see from our limited vantage point. That's why we believe in them; they provide us a glimpse into as well as the promise of eternity.

But is there room for ghosts in our supposedly materialistic, rationalistic world? Can the paranormal fit into this great mystery we call life, or must we jettison science and the realm of empirical knowledge in order to consider the idea?

Perhaps not. The universe is increasingly demonstrating itself to be a far more complex, mysterious, and wonderful place than we ever imagined. Whereas once we assumed we had a good understanding of what constituted reality, as we move into the twenty-first century, the boundaries of what was once considered empirical truth are being challenged all the time. Quantum physics, for one, continues to demonstrate on an almost daily basis that we are still in our infancy in terms of understanding the very nature of time and matter itself, making it easier than ever before to find room for the paranormal, the mysterious, and the apparently impossible to coexist alongside the proven, the testable, and the empirical.

But is science ready to listen? Perhaps in recognizing that it has had its house of cards knocked down too many times in the past will give it the humility to take a more objective look at the paranormal, and in so doing potentially afford us a golden opportunity to expand the boundaries of human understanding to never before imagined heights. Only time will tell.

However, before either science or we ourselves can begin to seriously consider the question of postmortem existence in earnest, there remains one major obstacle to overcome: while millions of people believe in ghosts, very few know more than a few basic things about them. And, worse, most of what we as a society have come to believe about the subject comes to us through sensationalized movies based far more on stereotypes and horror than on anything approaching cold, hard fact. While a handful of thoughtful movies have been produced, most Hollywood epics pander to the lowest common denominator of gore and horror with little thought given to the true complexities of the subject, which has had the unfortunate consequence of preventing science—or many people, for that matter—from taking a serious look at the issue of ghosts.

Thus the purpose of this book. It is not an effort to either prove or disprove the existence of ghosts, but an attempt to acquire a better perspective from which to seriously consider the issue and decide for ourselves whether it has anything to say to us. It is, after all, presumptuous to dismiss any concept without learning a few things about it first, and since the topic of life after death affects all of us in both subtle and significant ways, it would seem to deserve more than just a cursory glance. To that extent, what I have attempted to compile here is a brief compendium of theories and ideas held about ghosts that attempts to walk the narrow path between full-blown belief and cynical skepticism from the perspective of both one who is entirely comfortable with the idea of ghosts as well as from the standpoint of one who also recognizes how much fraud, foolishness, and nonsense has been a part of the ghost trade over the years.

Of course, some will find this attempt to walk such a narrow line to be a contradiction; after all, how can one be a believer and a skeptic at the same time and hope to do justice to either position?

While an excellent question and an objection that needs to be taken into account, it is also one that quickly evaporates once one understands that the term "skeptic" is not necessarily synonymous with "debunker." A debunker is one whose mind is already made up and who cannot permit even a modicum of objectivity to enter his or her field of vision, thus making him or her incapable of approaching the subject with fairness. The skeptic, on the other hand, is not burdened by such emotional baggage and so is free to question the evidence, not in an effort to dismiss it, but in the hope of better understanding it. It is the skeptics that push for natural explanations for apparently extraordinary events and uncover fraud whenever it is present, for they are the only ones truly capable of doing so. If they are honest in their quest, they will also be the first to point out that there may be much about the universe we don't yet understand or appreciate, and so they are willing to look at the data with some degree of humility, recognizing that however unlikely the idea of ghosts may be, there is always the possibility that such a thing does, in fact, exist.

As for myself, I would be less than honest if I tried to maintain I have no opinion on the matter. I have always been favorably inclined toward the idea that human consciousness survives death, and so have never entertained any serious objections to the idea of ghosts. That being said, however, I have also never personally seen one, so I can't claim to be an ardent believer either. I am fully aware of the human proclivity toward hysteria and wild imaginings—along with the pure fun of hoaxing—especially where the mysterious and paranormal are concerned, and so I approach every story with more than a little caution. Like most skeptics, I suspect that there are far more frivolous imaginings than genuine encounters going on out there. However, I also find it equally unlikely that every experience can be dismissed as mere hallucination, suggestion, or fraud; there are simply too many plausible stories being told by levelheaded, responsible people for *all* of them to be nonsense. That is just not the way the world works.

As such, I believe that in being neither a paranormal investigator on a quest to prove the existence of the supernatural nor a self-proclaimed champion of logic intent on debunking everything that seems silly to my way of thinking makes me uniquely qualified to put together a book like this. I genuinely have no stake in whether you believe or not; I only offer some ideas about what we are dealing with here, how investigators go about looking for these things, and some thoughts about what might be going on from a metaphysical standpoint. In the end I am content to leave it to the readers to decide for themselves if there is anything of value in this material and leave it at that.

Further, this book is not another collection of anecdotal stories that seem to so predominate the bookshelves nowadays, nor is it another "how to" book on ghost hunting. While I have great respect for those who take the time to painstakingly interview scores of witnesses or who make looking for evidence of the paranormal their life's passion,[1] that is not what this work is designed to do. This material is more theoretical in nature; my perspective being that of a curious outsider looking not for another good ghost story, but as one hoping to understand the phenomena of ghosts in a broader context. In effect, this is not a book about things that happened, but why they might happen and what it all means when they do.

As part of this quest, it will be necessary to take a brief look at the science and tools behind paranormal investigations, not in an effort to teach others how to stalk and bag their quarry like some big-game hunter, but in an effort to better understand how those who consider themselves ghost hunters go about the task of uncovering evidence of

---

1. For those who are interested in the minutia of paranormal research and investigation, however, I do include a few "how to" books in the bibliography.

otherworldly manifestations. The tools of the trade are vast and varied, and it helps to have a good working knowledge of how they function and what they are designed to do if we are to have a solid understanding of the subject, which I will endeavor to do in the following chapters. Additionally, as it has been my observation that some ghost enthusiasts have been entirely too anxious to believe everything they see and hear, much to the chagrin of honest and objective investigators whose efforts to achieve some degree of scientific credibility are frequently stymied by such naiveté, I will demonstrate how "frighteningly" easy it is to fake a ghost picture, as well as present photos of common photographic anomalies that are frequently mistaken for ghostly manifestations. This is not done in an effort to debunk the possibility that ghosts might be captured on film, but as a means of demonstrating how easy, especially in our age of sophisticated computer graphics, it is to make anything look convincing, as well as illustrate how some common photo aberrations and anomalies can convince even the most careful ghost hunters that they have captured a specter on film. Again, this is not done as a means of demonstrating how easily people can be fooled, but in an effort to underline why the serious investigator must be careful about accepting even the best evidence at face value. Skepticism, as long as it at least remains open to the possibility that the supernatural exists, is a valuable and even priceless commodity in the ghost-hunting game that can prevent one from being taken in by a cunning hoaxster and so risk losing potentially years' worth of hard-won credibility.

I will also make an effort to bring some consistency to a field of study that has been wrought with an often widely divergent terminology. Of course, many will reject my attempts to classify ghosts into various types or categories according to their scientific, spiritual, religious, and even psychological aspects as unnecessary or even simplistic, but it should at the very least allow us to recognize the remarkable complexity of the subject and afford us the opportunity to deconstruct some of the theories about ghosts currently in vogue. It is also my intention to put together a book that will ask the sort of questions "regular" people might ask. Some of these will be more psychological or even philosophical in nature, but such questions are important ones to ask, for I am convinced that ghosts have much to tell us about ourselves and the universe around us if we will only take the time to better understand what makes them "tick." Examples of questions that rotate around these ideas might be as prosaic as whether everyone becomes a ghost or is it a fate only some people are destined to endure; to whether one becomes a ghost by choice or are ghosts trapped here against their will (and if they can leave whenever they wish, where might they go)? Other, questions, however, will be more scientific in nature and will deal with the intriguing aspects of energy and the power of the mind to create and manifest itself under ideal circumstances. To this effect, we will look into the questions of to what degree a ghost might interact within the linear world of time and space, how they might be able to do so, and why a ghost would choose to haunt a particular location in the first place. We will also look at things like poltergeists and ask ourselves if they really are "noisy ghosts" or whether they are a manifestation of unconscious telekinetic energy. We will even look at the question of whether ghostly manifestations can really be imprinted into the environment of a house, or if there may not be other explanations for the phenomenon of repeating apparitions, as well as consider other ghostly phenomena from a rationalist perspective.

Additionally, since I wanted to put together a book that dealt with the full range of potential paranormal activity, I am devoting a couple of chapters to theories having to do with malevolent spirits and what we popularly refer to as demons. This is an area of study I have rarely found addressed in any detail in most books of this type, largely due, I think, to the discomfort most people feel when discussing the potentially darker side of the supernatural, but one that needs to be dealt with as well, especially considering the potential danger such entities, if they indeed exist, could pose. As part of this study, we will also look specifically at the phenomena of demonic possession, another area some readers may find either silly or disturbing—depending upon their cultural inclinations—but one I think important to look at, not only for what it might tell us about the paranormal in general, but for what it can tell us about the power of suggestion and how our cultural beliefs may impact our day-to-day reality. Unfortunately, while my intent was to keep this as secular a book as possible, I do not think it is possible to fully appreciate the phenomenon of demonic possession without understanding the role religion plays in it. To try and do so would be like trying to understand the solar system without recognizing the profound role gravity has in holding it all together. As such, since religion and the concept of evil are profoundly linked, this will necessitate my going off on a few religious tangents on occasion, for which I hope the reader will forgive me.

Finally, we will look at some ideas having to do with the controversial subject of contacting ghosts and other supernatural entities, such as spirit guides, angels, and messengers. We will explore various forms of spirit communication, how mediumship supposedly works, whether things like Ouija boards and automatic writing could serve as legitimate conduits for spiritual communication, and how one might communicate with spiritual energies personally. In this I will be forced to interject a few ideas and personal experiences of my own into the mix in an effort to better explain how such communication might not only be possible, but even beneficial, in the hope that readers will find these experiences helpful in understanding the nature of spirit communication as well as useful in understanding how to pursue their own relations with these beings themselves, if they so desire.

Obviously, much of what we will discuss in these few chapters will lie well outside the realm of the provable and perhaps—to some readers—even outside the veil of reason, but a subject like ghosts is nothing if not an invitation to speculate and hypothesize. Such is, after all, the foundation upon which knowledge is advanced and refined. Further, I am fully aware that in the end it is likely that even the best evidence will not convince those intent on disbelief, nor the best rationalist arguments sway the true believer into taking a second look, but at least we will retain the right to judge for ourselves those things that speak to us, which is our right and duty as free-thinking human beings.

With these ground rules in place then, we are ready to embark upon our journey of discovery, which is, after all, is the only journey life presents us that is truly worth taking. I hope you will find it both a fascinating and thought provoking trip, and one that will instill in you a desire to more fully explore the mysteries that exist all around us. All it takes is an open mind and the recognition that none of us has a corner on understanding the vast intricacies of the universe; hopefully, that will be enough to make our quest an enjoyable one, and one that will bring us to a greater appreciation of the mysterious world we all share.

part one

Laying the Groundwork

No phenomenon can be fully appreciated or studied without some context within which to understand it, and ghosts are no exception. As such, it is necessary to begin our journey by first constructing a foundation upon which to consider the subject of the paranormal in general and ghosts in particular.

To do this, it is first important to ask ourselves some very basic questions. First and foremost, we need to consider the question of postmortem existence itself, for without some basis by which we might accept the possibility that human consciousness could survive the death of the body that sustains it, any further discussion about ghosts becomes irrelevant. To do that requires not only an understanding of how science in general looks upon the issue of immortality, but how it might be possible for human consciousness to exist in some context outside that of flesh and blood.

To do this, however, it will be necessary to carefully examine such concepts as the soul, the definition of consciousness, personality, sentience, and other metaphysical constructs such as precisely what a ghost is, how it might operate within the context of both the supernatural and physical realms, why and how someone might become a ghost, and what eventually becomes of these otherworldly entities over time. While this will inevitably force us to resort to a great deal of speculation, such is to be expected. After all, this book isn't about proving the existence of ghosts, but in defining them in the hopes of learning not just more about them, but, more importantly, about ourselves.

chapter one

The Science of Disbelief

Many people struggle under the misconception that it is the job of science to disprove the existence of ghosts. Nothing, however, could be further from the truth.

It is not science's job to explain everything away as tricks of light and shadow, or to demonstrate the ability of the human brain to trick itself into believing all sorts of strange things. Science, in fact, is under absolutely no obligation at all to explain away every ghostly image caught on film or demonstrate how a fraud was perpetrated, nor is it required to demonstrate a Ouija board to be nothing more than a superfluous toy for the easily entertained.

Instead, it is the task of the paranormal investigators to prove the existence of the phenomena they are studying, which is the way it should be. It is they who must weather science's best efforts at destroying every hypothesis and theory, for that is science's job. It is specifically designed to destroy, not reinforce, new theories; its role being to test ideas according to certain fixed and rigid standards and destroy those that do not make the grade. One only needs to examine the past to find examples of its handiwork and, conversely, see how those theories that survived the process went on to be enshrined within the very foundations of human understanding.

Of course, the parapsychologist faces a more daunting challenge than most scientists, for he is already handicapped by the fact that science dismisses the idea of ghosts outright and even generally refuses to acknowledge the paranormal as a legitimate field of study. This is because science is dogmatically naturalistic in its perceptions of the universe and so considers all phenomenon to be explainable through natural, as opposed to supernatural, processes. It does not easily accept concepts like the survival of human consciousness or the existence of the soul, which obviously leaves things like ghosts out in the cold. Not surprisingly, then, the handful of qualified and credentialed parapsychologists brave enough to actually research the subject are usually dismissed as clever but misguided individuals who are wasting their talents in the pursuit of what could only be described as "junk" science, which has the natural consequence of forcing paranormal investigators to not only work harder to prove themselves but results in standards of what constitutes proof to be significantly tougher than for other sciences. In effect, the bar is set higher for the paranormal investigator than it is for nearly any other researcher and, further, as technology improves, that bar is being continually raised, making the paranormal one of the few scientific disciplines for which the standards of proof may remain almost always just beyond the reach of even the most determined investigator.

Some might say it is unfair of science to demand more from the parapsychologist than it does from any other scientist, but that is a matter of personal perspective. After all, the belief in an afterlife and, by extension, ghosts is considered an extraordinary claim that demands extraordinary evidence. Further, it is not science that has infected the entire field of study with centuries worth of superstition, fraud, quackery, and nonsense, so it seems only fair that more evidence than usual be demanded for a field of study that, were it ever to be proven, would dramatically alter our worldview and shake the very foundations of science itself. The stakes are astronomically high, and since they impact every man, woman, and child on this planet in profound ways, an even more skeptical approach than usual seems prudent.

But science needs to be careful as well, for in its ruthless quest to ascertain truth, it occasionally becomes victimized by its own intransigence. More than once it has been unwilling to consider new ideas even when the evidence appeared to be overwhelmingly in favor of them, resulting in needless suffering and even death. For those whose faith in science is such that they can't imagine such a possibility, we need only go back a couple of centuries to see one of the greatest examples of how not to pursue the truth. Hopefully, it should give even the most skeptical reader pause as we consider the evidence for ghosts.

The Germ Theory Debate

Throughout much of its history and well into the early nineteenth century, medical science believed that sickness was caused by poisoned blood and other impurities in the systems and that the best way to treat serious illness was by bleeding and purging the patient of these impurities in the hopes that the body, no longer forced to battle the accumulated poisons massing within it, would finally rally and find the strength to recover. The practice, which was considered sound medical practice for centuries, led not only to much needless suffering, but in denying the body the vital antibodies needed to fight infection (as well as contributing to dehydration by depriving the patient of vital body fluids), it made the chances of succumbing to illness not only more likely but, in some cases, even inevitable.

While there are numerous examples of how destructive this procedure was, perhaps one of the more famous instances is that of the first president of the United States and Revolutionary War general George Washington. Catching a case of laryngitis after riding his horse on a cold December day in 1799, over the next few days his illness evolved into full-blown pneumonia. Several of the finest doctors of his day were brought in, but despite their best efforts at saving the beloved president's life, his condition worsened and he died just a few days before Christmas, much to the great shock of the young country. Though officially it is recorded that Washington died of pneumonia, it should be noted that his demise was likely hastened by the fact that his doctors took great pains to ensure that he was bled frequently, during which as much as a quarter pint of "poisoned blood" was purged from his system each time. While there is no evidence Washington would have survived without this procedure being done, it is almost certain his chances of recovery were greatly reduced by his being subjected to it.

Of course, no one at the time imagined it was the efforts of the attending physicians that posed the greatest threat to the president. Bleeding was an accepted and standard medical practice of the day and, as such, it, along with a number of other dubious and usually ineffective procedures, continued to be practiced for decades afterward, undoubtedly resulting in even more unnecessary (or greatly hastened) deaths. Remarkably, its effectiveness as a means of restoring health was never seriously questioned and, in fact, doctors were frequently even applauded for their heroic efforts at attempting to save their patients by bleeding them to death.[2]

During the mid-nineteenth century, however, French chemist and microbiologist Louis Pasteur, along with a few others, hypothesized that it was not poisoned blood and bile that was responsible for most disease, but microorganisms that he called germs that were the culprit. He proposed that creatures too small to be seen with the naked eye (and, in most cases, too small to be seen with the best instruments of the day) were ubiquitous within the human body and that it was when they became too numerous that sickness resulted. Further, in a complete reversal of standard medical thinking of the day, he hypothesized that there was no such thing as poisoned blood at all but that it was the blood itself that was the very agent responsible for keeping these tiny organisms in check. In fact, it was in bleeding the patient that the real danger lay, for it robbed the victim of the very antibacterial properties needed to kill these tiny organisms, thus hastening the demise doctors were attempting to circumvent. In essence, Pasteur maintained nothing less than that medical science had it all wrong and was, in fact, even making matters worse.

---

2. Obviously, this was made possible by assuming that any patient who survived being bled and recovered was saved by the procedure, while those that did not survive were thought to have too much poisoned blood to make bleeding effective. In neither case, however, was the efficacy of the procedure itself ever brought into question.

Not surprisingly, these ideas did not make Pasteur a particularly popular man. Almost overnight he saw his hypothesis rejected as bizarre nonsense by the established medical community and himself the subject of scorn and ridicule by many of his learned colleagues. Undaunted, however, and determined to prove his hypothesis correct, he put together a number of experiments that ultimately demonstrated that such creatures did, in fact, exist and that the established medical practice of bleeding was not only useless in curing disease, but actually detrimental to it.

Remarkably, however, even after the weight of the evidence continued to pile up and despite the work of later scientists such as Lister and Koch that demonstrated the link between tuberculosis and other diseases to airborne organisms and the value of antiseptics in reducing or preventing infection, it still took years for Pasteur's theories to win acceptance. It took even more time for the medical community to change its practices to incorporate it on a regular basis, further dooming millions to needlessly die from easily preventable infection (for example, hand washing prior to surgery or childbirth was still not commonly practiced until late in the nineteenth century, frequently resulting in septic infection and easily avoidable death). Eventually, however, science accepted germ theory as fact and, with it, was able to lay the foundation for modern medical science. Pasteur's work, then, not only saved lives but may have saved medical science itself—a sobering thought if one considers it carefully.

Of course, it is easy to shake our heads at the ignorance and naiveté of centuries-old medicine and believe that we are too enlightened to make the same mistake today, but can we really be so certain? After all, consider the effect something as unusual as germ theory would have had on the scientific mind-set of the early nineteenth century: that illness was the product of creatures that conveniently happened to be too small to be seen with the naked eye and whose existence could only be surmised seemed a bit too convenient and even preposterous. Further, it seemed an unnecessarily complex answer to the question of why people grew sick and died, and was considered a pointless debate in any case when science had, on the surface at least, been successfully dealing with disease through the established and traditional method of bleeding for centuries. Further, so much of Pasteur's theory had to be taken on faith. The microscope was still years away from being powerful enough to reveal microscopic organisms, and his idea that such creatures existed outside the ability of our five senses to detect them was purely conjectural. It seemed too fantastic, too irrational, and a far too complex and unwieldy explanation for what was happening, so it is not difficult to understand why Pasteur met such resistance. Additionally, decades of training and experience, not to mention hard-earned professional credentials, would be jeopardized if Pasteur's theories proved correct, so is it really so inexplicable that men of good conscience were hostile to the idea? Are we really so different today?

Fortunately, Pasteur and the other pioneers in the field didn't accept the conventional thinking on the subject, and their discoveries (along with the persistence that made them possible) are not only what made modern medicine possible, but are what permits us to live far healthier and longer lives today. In the end Pasteur and a handful of colleagues demonstrated that while orthodox thinking and refusing to challenge the established dogma of the day may have made for long, full careers, it is only through unconventional thinking and a willingness to take chances that our knowledge expands.

Modern-Day Germ Theory

Perhaps the same is true of the paranormal today. Just as germ theory was the great nonsense of nineteenth-century science, so too may ghosts be the modern equivalent of Pasteur's revolutionary hypothesis. Just as bacterium did in Pasteur's day, so too may ghosts lie just beyond our five senses, and though they can be sometimes seen and heard and even supposedly recorded on modern equipment, we must lie in wait for more modern and sophisticated tools to expose them. Like Pasteur, we too may have to wait for the equivalent of the electron microscope to be perfected before we can one day detect our quarry in an empirical manner. Until then, however, ghosts must remain just on the periphery of proof, taunting us to look closer and keep trying, implying that their secrets can be ours if only we don't give up the fight, all the while remaining stubbornly resistant to even the most determined efforts to locate that one example of incontrovertible evidence that might settle the issue. It can be a frustrating endeavor, especially in the face of a scientific community that generally considers all such efforts to be unworthy of serious study and quickly labels all such research as pseudoscience at best. Pasteur would have understood the feeling.

There is some good news, however. Today we live in an age when the means to unlock the mystery of the supernatural may be within our grasp. Just as it wasn't until technology had advanced sufficiently that it was possible to even hypothesize the existence of microscopic organisms, so too we may just now be getting to that same point where the concept of ghosts and the survivability of human consciousness is concerned. Technology may finally be bringing us to the threshold of an exciting new era in which we can expand beyond the world of the five senses to explore the entirely unique and never-before-imagined realms that may lie just outside of the rigid confines of empirical science.

Unfortunately, while this brave new world of the paranormal promises to expand humanity's vision, how is it possible to seriously study a subject that is so riddled with superstition, imagination, and outright fraud? Poorly staged seances and crudely manipulated photos have done much to damage the historical credibility of the issue, while in modern times the dismal record of many self-styled ghost hunters and incompetent enthusiasts have prevented even the most promising leads from being taken seriously. For every solid piece of evidence that suggests there is more going on than science might like to admit, there are a hundred bits of nonsense parading as proof of the supernatural. Is it any wonder, then, that the idea of ghosts is also met with such scorn and ridicule by the scientific community? As such, it seems the quest is stymied even before it begins, for not only is the paranormal investigator beset by science's firmly entrenched skepticism, but it is being forced to carry the accumulated baggage of centuries of quackery and superstition as well.

Further, the job is made even more difficult by the unpredictability of the very phenomenon they are trying to study. Ghosts are seldom predictable, repeatable, testable, or even verifiable, so the task of proving their existence is a formidable one. Yet there is some reason for optimism. Not only has the technology vastly improved over the years, but so has the quality of the research being conducted. Whereas once just a few anecdotal stories were sufficient to be considered evidence of a haunting, now the standards of what constitutes evidence is much higher. Additionally, the availability of photo manipulation techniques and other technologies have made the investigator far more wary than ever before, for the serious researcher knows only too well how easily evidence can be faked. Long gone are the days when a few blurred snapshots were enough to be seriously considered as evidence; today even the best too-good-to-be-true photos are carefully scrutinized by an army of experts, each hoping to be the first to expose how it was faked. Whereas once stories told by the most eccentric and unscrupulous persons were believed without question, today even the most credible witnesses are carefully examined, not only for flaws in their story but in their character as well. Of course, there is still the occasional charlatan, the incompetent researcher, and the just plain naïve hobbyist out there to contend with—such people have always been, and will probably always remain, a part of all scientific endeavor—yet today such people are finding it increasingly difficult to carry the day as they once did.

Yet even if the technology and the standards of evidence are improving, that does not mean proof of postmortem existence is necessarily on the horizon. In fact, it may never come, yet it is important the effort to find it still be attempted, for it is only in pushing the envelope of knowledge that anything approaching proof is even theoretically possible. Even if the belief in life after death remains nothing more than a hope and an article of faith, it still needs to be explored if only for the potential treasure of understanding and enlightenment it promises to afford us. After all, an "x" marked on a treasure map remains nothing more than a foolish bit of nonsense only as long as there is no real treasure to uncover.

Finally, consider what science would be losing if human consciousness does survive the grave and it missed it. It would mean missing the opportunity to better understand our own place in the cosmos and allow us to reinterpret our world in a completely new way. We would no longer be brief and momentary participants in one species' attempt to survive, but would instead become immortal players in a cosmic process of growth and knowledge. It seems such a possibility might be worth taking a few risks or, at a minimum, reserving final judgment. Isn't it too important to do otherwise?

chapter two

The Case for Immortality

Before we can begin examining the subject of ghosts in earnest, it is first necessary to establish a premise from which to begin our journey, and that has been and remains the supposition that the human personality survives the death of the physical body that houses it. If we cannot establish that as at least a theoretical possibility, any further discussion of ghosts—at least as a manifestation of non-corporeal human consciousness—is pointless. As such, in this chapter we will attempt to establish a rational hypothesis by which the human personality might conceivably survive death, thereby providing us with some basis upon which to continue our discussion.

Of course, to a large degree the belief that the personality (that which we might call the soul or spirit of a human being) survives the demise of the physical body must remain an article of faith, but then so is the supposition that it does not. This is not simply a case of faith versus evidence but, to a large degree, a clear-cut challenge to the materialist assumption that death constitutes the end of existence. The paranormal field of study in general and such things as ghosts, past-life memories (reincarnation), and near death experiences (NDEs) all threaten that assumption, and since science works from the premise that one shouldn't believe that which cannot be empirically proven, conflict is inevitable. It is nothing less than the very basic perception of what constitutes reality that is at stake here, with both sides having

much to lose should the weight of evidence tumble in their opponent's favor.

Since it is probably impossible to adequately demonstrate that the
human personality survives the death of the brain to everyone's satisfaction, however, I will not attempt to do so here. It is beyond the ability of any mere book to prove such a premise in any case, so I will not
pretend to be any more capable of settling the issue than anyone else.
However, there are some basic ideas that can be presented that might
at least induce the skeptic to consider the possibility that the human
personality is immortal. If I can simply show why those who believe in
life after death can hold to such an opinion on a rational basis, a dialogue becomes theoretically possible, which is, at least, a good place to
start.

Defining Consciousness

Before proceeding, it is first necessary to more precisely define what it
is we are looking for here. What is it, exactly, that is supposed to survive death to manifest as a ghost?

It is generally assumed that what survives death and serves as the
basis for a paranormal manifestation is what we call consciousness or,
more precisely, a person's individual personality. However, this is
where it begins to get tricky, for while consciousness is an element of
the personality, not all consciousness necessarily possesses personality.
Additionally, consider that even the term consciousness is one that
can be rather loosely defined to mean different things to different
people. For some, consciousness is defined in fairly broad terms as the
capacity of a brain to function on some level, which essentially makes
almost all living organisms essentially conscious. This makes the term
synonymous with life; to be conscious, then, is to be alive or, at the
very least, an animate object.

This definition, however, presents an immediate problem, for there
are many things we would consider alive that do not possess consciousness, at least as we would define the term. Plants, for example,

are alive, as are things like single-celled organisms and viruses, yet they would not normally be considered conscious. As such, the idea of where, precisely, one defines the point at which basic life ends and consciousness begins can be a difficult one and a point open to serious discussion.

Others, however, define consciousness in a much broader context. When metaphysicists talk in terms of human consciousness, it is generally understood to mean more than just the essence of a living thing, but the byproduct of the higher brain functions that gives us our unique characteristics and makes us a distinct, one-of-a-kind individual. It is that which gives us the ability to produce tools or build a fire or, for that matter, create art and literature, manufacture goods or even develop religion, that they are talking about. It is also that which makes it possible for us to appreciate a good meal, find joy in the company of others, marvel at a magnificent sunset, or even find mystery in the stars. It is what gives us self-awareness, an appreciation for beauty, the need for love, and the ability to look beyond ourselves to ponder our place in a much larger universe. In essence, it is that part of ourselves that makes us a unique, distinct, and individualized part of a greater whole, and that is the element of ourselves that may not only be able to transcend the very brain that houses it, but may, in fact, be capable of surviving apart from it.

And here is where the battle lines are drawn, for the materialist[3] will ask, quite rightly, why should this one aspect of the brain—or any element of it, for that matter—be capable of surviving the death of the brain? Why do we imagine that our rational processes, likes and dislikes, memories, sense of humor (everything that makes us distinctly and uniquely us) should survive when the lower byproducts of the brain—the autonomic reflexes, instincts, and raw intelligence—clearly do not? It seems that if these elements are unable to exist apart from those few pounds of gray mush that are currently enclosed within the

---

3. A materialist being defined here not as a person who finds pleasure in acquiring material possessions, but as one who believes that matter and energy are all that exists in the universe and that all processes and phenomena can be explained through natural laws without metaphysical explanations being either necessary or desirable.

bony mantle of our skull, then once that dies, all that which we call personality must also die, or so logic would seem to dictate.

That, in effect, is the bulk of the argument. As long as our personality remains a purely internalized biochemical byproduct of firing neurons, there is no reason to imagine it would have any more ability to survive death than would our libido. Such does appear to constitute a powerful rationale against the idea of postmortem existence and presents a simple argument that seemingly slams the door on the possibility of ghosts even before it can be opened.

However, I wonder if it is really that simple.

Finding the Source of Personality

Could the higher functions of the brain transcend the organ that gives them life, or do we exist only within the cells of an imperfect (and increasingly failing) organ we call the brain? It seems the entire argument of whether there are such things as ghosts hinges on this very point, and so we must do our best to try to answer it.

To find an answer, it is first necessary to question where human personality comes from in the first place. It is generally assumed it originates from within the brain as a byproduct of the bioelectrical impulses that make this marvelous piece of circuitry function. It is further shaped and transformed over the life of a person by its environment, experiences, and conditioning, making it nothing more than the byproduct of the cells that make up the brain and a reflection of the wider environment that brain finds itself in.

If so, however, that brings up an interesting question: how is it possible that something which is not in and of itself intelligent or self-aware—the cells of the human brain—can collectively create that which is intelligent and self-aware? In other words, where do the individual cells that make up the brain acquire the consciousness that makes personality possible in the first place? Isn't this a case of getting something from nothing?

This problem is further compounded when we consider that on the subatomic level the atoms that make up our brain are not at all that different from those that make up every other thing that exists in the universe. For example, the brain and a diamond are both composed, to a large degree, of carbon atoms. In fact, if you took a carbon atom from your brain and compared it to a carbon atom from a diamond drill bit, you would find no difference between them at all; they would be identical in all respects. However, no one would claim that a diamond, despite being densely packed with carbon atoms, is alive or that it possesses a mind. Therefore, why do the same atoms, when encased within the cells of the human brain, appear to be not only self-aware and conscious, but capable of doing things like writing a book or playing a guitar?

Further, consider that each atom, of which a single brain cell contains many billions, are composed of subatomic particles of energy adrift in an ocean of empty space, not unlike our own solar system. In fact, each atom is a microcosm of our solar system, with the particles that circle the nucleus proportionately the same distance from that nucleus as Jupiter is from our own sun. In other words, just as our own solar system is 99.999 percent empty space, so too are the atoms in our brain mostly empty space (giving new meaning to the term "airhead," one would imagine). Yet from this vast universe of nothingness comes music and literature and philosophy and science, leading us to wonder how these little, empty, mindless atoms do it. Does this not at least suggest that the mind may not be the creation of subatomic particles, but conceivably exists apart from them? Otherwise, it truly does seem to be a case of creating something—or, for that matter, everything—from nothing!

Clearly there is more to the mind than the cumulative electrical impulses of trillions of atoms. And since we can find no evidence that atoms and the other things that make up the brain are inherently self-aware and sentient in and of themselves, it suggests that the mind or, on a more basic level, consciousness, must reside somewhere else outside of the brain. If true, however, this has profound implications, for in implying that consciousness exists outside of ourselves, it also suggests that the mind may not be so much the product of subatomic particles, but that subatomic particles are the "stuff" consciousness uses to bring itself into existence, which it does by creating a mechanism—the brain—to serve as the means by which that consciousness can manifest itself within the physical realm. In other words, *the brain may be a product of the mind rather than the mind a product of the brain.*

This forces us to look at the brain in a completely different light and see it not as a thought transmitter but as a thought receiver. Obviously, this is a metaphysical concept, but one that needs to be considered if we are to find any basis by which the human personality might survive death and potentially manifest itself within the physical realm.

The Brain as a Receiver

Most people understand how radio and television sets work: a transmission station beams a signal into space that is eventually picked up by a distant receiver set to the proper frequency. The receiver does not create the signal, of course, but merely intercepts it and amplifies it into some form we can understand (through our auditory and visual senses). In the same way then, just as a radio signal exists apart from the receiver that captures it, so too we might speculate that consciousness, playing the role of the invisible, formless radio wave, is captured and interpreted by the solid, material receiver we call the brain, which picks up the signal and gives it form.

If true, this has enormous repercussions. Foremost among them, it suggests that just as the destruction of every radio and television receiver in the world would not destroy the radio and television signals they are attempting to intercept (which will continue to fly off into space forever, irrespective of whether anyone is tuning in or not), so too would the destruction or death of the brain have no effect upon the existence of the intelligence that is using that brain to manifest itself. Instead, it will continue to exist, potentially forever, completely apart from the brain that once housed it.

Additionally, since consciousness might theoretically exist apart from a brain just as a radio wave exists apart from a receiver, it implies that consciousness may be ubiquitous throughout the universe. As such, just as a radio broadcast originating from a single studio is picked up by literally thousands of receivers simultaneously, consciousness itself might be broadcasting itself in all directions continually, waiting to be picked up by various receivers—of which our brain may be just one type—scattered throughout the universe.

It is an interesting possibility that says much about how human personality might conceivably survive the demise of the very brain that gives it substance. It survives for the very simple reason that just as a radio transmitter is not dependent upon a receiver for its existence, the mind is not dependent upon a brain for its existence. In essence, it is the brain that exists because of the mind, not the other way around. It also suggests that just as a signal from a far-off star system might be many decades or even centuries old by the time we hear it, so too might the consciousness that manifests itself within our brain have existed long before we were even born. Essentially, if consciousness exists apart from our brain, it could be far older than the body that houses it, which, if true, suggests that consciousness may not only be prevalent and universal, but potentially eternal and ageless and, most important of all, immortal.

The Universal Consciousness

Obviously, I'm suggesting that if consciousness exists outside of the physical realm, it must be much larger and older than anyone can imagine. In fact, it could even be part of a single, massive, unified field of consciousness of which our manifestation in this body of flesh and blood is just one tiny expression. Of course, such a universal consciousness is only one small step away from God, but that is another issue entirely and not necessary for our purposes. It is all simply a matter of how one wishes to understand this larger, collective consciousness that is the issue; how or even if we might relate to it on some personal level is another question entirely.

However, this idea does present us with one small dilemma in that if we are all part of a single, universal consciousness, why do we not all possess identical personalities? After all, each radio receiver picks up and replays the identical broadcast, so it stands to reason that each brain that manifests a piece of this larger consciousness should manifest the same personality as well. However, we see that this is not the case; personalities are varied and rich in nuances, talents, perceptions, and abilities, so how can they all generate from the same source?

One possible answer is that this universal consciousness is so vast that no single brain can manifest more than one tiny aspect of it. Additionally, as each person is subjected to widely divergent environments, experiences, and circumstances that shape the resultant personality in various ways, each manifestation of universal consciousness is a unique and distinct experience for each receiver, despite finding its source in the same universal transmission. This is comparable to wood from the same tree being used to create a myriad of useful and distinctly different items. One person carves a spoon or a bowl, while another uses the wood from the same tree to make furniture or a door for their home. What final form the wood takes is a result of human will and need, but that does not detract from the fact that it shares the forest in common with all wooden objects.

Survival of the Lower Functions

If we are willing to consider the possibility that the source of personality lies outside ourselves and the cells that make up our brain are simply a kind of receiver capable of tuning into this greater universal personality, then what of the lower brain functions, such as the autonomic functions and things like instinct and basic intelligence? If the higher functions are capable of surviving, shouldn't the "lower" functions survive as well?

This is where it gets tricky, for while it's entirely possible that some universal constant is at work maintaining the lower brain functions in much the same way that the cosmic mind is giving the higher brain functions animation, there seems to be a difference between them. The lower functions are designed purely to keep an organism alive or "in the flesh," so to speak; as such, once it dies these functions are no longer required and they dissipate. This is why insects, fish, and plants are not believed to survive their own demise: they simply exist on too primitive a level for anything of substance to survive. The atoms that compose their nervous systems may have been receiving instructions from some external force that gave them the means to function in their designed venues, but once they were no longer needed the "receivers" shut down and the atoms that make up the dead organism eventually are reclaimed by the universe, to ultimately take on some new form, with new instructions and new assignments to carry out.

However, this seems not to be the case for those atoms that are carrying out the higher brain functions, for they have produced something more than just life or physicality. They have produced something greater than the sum of their parts, something unique and distinct and, as such, worth preserving. Therefore, since there is something more than just autonomic functions and basic instincts in residence, their byproduct would continue to survive, not in the physical realm but elsewhere, even long after the atoms of the brain that housed it have been reclaimed by the universe.

This computer I'm typing on is an excellent example of how this process may work. Consider that a great deal of my computer's memory is required simply to permit it to operate properly. Countless millions of instructions are being sent through its circuitry every minute, all designed to maintain its functionality, without which I would be incapable of typing a single word. However, the words themselves do not originate with the computer, but are a product of something outside itself—namely, me. As such, once I've completed a chapter, I can move that information onto a disk or send it to my printer, where it will be preserved as long as I wish to preserve it. If I were to take it one step further and have my computer networked into a central server where every bit of information in it is stored in some external electronic medium, the words I write would be safe were something to happen to my computer's hard drive or the circuits themselves otherwise damaged in some way. As such, even if my computer's circuitry was to become fried by a power surge, the information that was a byproduct of that circuitry would live on and would continue to exist elsewhere in complete form, no longer dependent upon the machine that built it to sustain it.

In the same way, then, the personality needs a brain to bring it into being, but it does not require one to maintain that existence after it has emerged. Where it goes exactly and what happens to it is a source of debate, but the possibility that it still exists must at least be considered.

Of course, this brings up the question of how conscious something needs to be before it is considered worthy of postmortem existence. In effect, could the conscious energy of certain higher animals also survive death to manifest itself as a ghost and, if not, why not?

That's where the whole issue of sentience comes into play. We simply do not know whether the most intelligent animals possess what we would know as sentience or personality. Certainly family pets have been known to exhibit widely divergent levels of aggression and affection, and dolphins and elephants, to name but two examples, do seem to have strongly developed social skills and to even be capable of rudimentary language, but it is uncertain whether these traits demonstrate them to be self-aware or "sentient." Perhaps they do, or perhaps in the case of animals there is something called a collective personality; a sense in which all dogs are part of a larger canine ethos, for example, but not unique enough to maintain an individual personality. On the other hand, it may simply be that animals don't care about such things as much as people do, forcing us to wonder which is the more advanced life-form.

Conclusion

If we work from the premise that consciousness and, with it, human personality is potentially capable of existing apart from the brain in the same way a radio wave can exist apart from a radio receiver, then we can only guess as to what capabilities that consciousness might possess outside of the physical realm. In fact, consciousness itself may be responsible for the very existence of the physical realm, in which case its ability to manipulate matter and energy might well be a natural part of its essence.

If so, then if an individual personality, be it living or dead, is an element of the overall universal consciousness that keeps the physical realm intact, this same energy—perhaps existing in the form of an invisible "cloud" of pure thought after death—should be theoretically capable of manifesting itself within the realm of time and space at any point and in many different ways. Why it would do so is another question, of course, but that it might at least be capable of choosing to manifest within the physical realm seems a reasonable premise, and one that, now equipped with at least a viable working hypothesis, we can explore in more depth.

Of course, I realize that much of this is based on several major assumptions, but it does attempt to account for how a personality might survive the physical demise of its own body. I doubt if it will sway the most determined materialist, but it should make it more difficult to ignore the possibility that the human personality might survive death. It is simply a matter of reducing the material world to its most basic parts and then asking a few questions about where those parts got their intelligence, wisdom, talent, and abilities. In doing so, we may discover that the worlds of matter and of spirit may not be as far apart as many people imagine. In fact, we might even discover that they are all a part of the same basic stuff, an idea that seems capable of turning our understanding of the nature of reality on its collective head. While this may not make for sound science, it does make for a universe brimming with remarkable possibilities, of which things like ghosts may be but one of many.

chapter three

Defining a Ghost

Having established at least a basis by which we might concede the possibility that consciousness can survive death, we are now in a position where we can begin to answer the basic questions, such as just what, exactly, are ghosts and how do they operate? And, for that matter, are there different types of ghosts or are all ghosts basically the same?

Before we move on, however, this might be a good place to establish a basic terminology of ghost hunting, which will prove invaluable in helping us better define our quarry. While this process of pigeonholing everything into neat little categories is a common and characteristically human failing, it is unfortunately necessary. Even when scientists disagree among themselves as to the validity of a particular phenomenon, they have generally been very careful about at least articulating precisely what the phenomenon in question is. For instance, individuals may disagree as to whether extraterrestrials have visited Earth in the past, but we can all at least agree on what constitutes an extraterrestrial. As such, it is necessary we establish a basic language of the paranormal if we are to get anywhere in our discussion. Unfortunately, being that "ghost hunting" is such a largely new and as yet unrecognized field of science, precise definitions of even the most basic paranormal phenomena are often subjective. It has been my observation that even a term as apparently self-explanatory as "ghost" often means very different things to different people. To some, a ghost and an entity are interchangeable terms, while others define a ghost purely as a nonconscious manifestation of a past living person (often also referred to as an imprint) and define an interactive disembodied personality as an entity. Then there are those who reject the word ghost entirely, preferring manifestation, apparition, specter, or even the quasi-religious term spirit instead, thus further muddying the metaphysical waters. This process is further complicated not just by variations in terminology, but by the fact that not all ghosts are apparently human. There are numerous accounts of spectral animals, nonhuman energies (so-called angels and demons), and even inanimate objects such as trains or ships to contend with, making it even more difficult to create a one-size-fits-all definition of just what a ghost is.

Nonetheless, we must still try to develop some set definitions from which to work, if only for the sake of clarity. Of course, I recognize that my efforts at bringing order to the process is no more definitive than anyone else's, but I do believe mine to be at least an honest effort at finding some consensus among the various paranormal camps, as well as an attempt to bring some degree of consistency and internal logic to the process. I am sure some readers, particularly those who are already "old hands" on the subject, may find many of my definitions to be questionable and will continue to insist upon their own preferred terminology, which is fine; I only offer these as a reasonable place to start, not the final word on the subject.

The Interactive Personality

The first and probably most commonly accepted definition of a ghost is the disembodied energy of a deceased human being that appears not only self-aware, but quite capable of interacting within the linear world of time and space. These interactions may include making itself visible to the naked eye, being able to communicate (either audibly or telepathically), and even being capable of touching and, on rare occasions, of being touched by the living. These types of manifestations have even been known to possess the ability to manufacture odors that were associated with their human host when they were alive (such as tobacco, perfume, or aftershave), making them apparently capable of operating within the full spectrum of our five natural human senses (and, potentially, even our sixth sense). Further, just as human beings are capable of displaying a wide range of emotions and temperaments, so too do ghosts. In fact, they seem to retain much of their former personality, making them remarkably human in many ways. Some may be playful and loving while others are dark and angry. Often they are described as brooding, sad, or melancholy, and are frequently observed exhibiting such very human emotions as rage, fear, and jealousy. As such, an encounter with such an entity may be either pleasant or frightening, depending upon the nature and temperament of the ghost and the circumstances of its manifestation (as well as the emotional state of the observer). In general, however, most interactive personalities are considered harmless and, in some cases, even beneficial and should be treated with the respect and dignity accorded to any human being, be they living or dead.

Since such types of ghosts apparently retain much, if not all, of their former earthbound personality, be it positive or negative, and are capable of feeling emotions, I think a better term for a non-corporeal or disembodied consciousness that is clearly human in origin should be a *personality* rather than either entity or the more generalized term ghost. *Personality* captures the essence of what this being is; it is a person who simply no longer resides within the context (and, some might say, the confines) of the physical body. As such, to identify such a presence as a *personality* is simply to acknowledge its inherent humanity.

Personalities are further divided into several subcategories, each of which are largely determined by their relationship to the viewer. Those of a recognized family member or friend who has passed are called *familial personalities* because they are intimately familiar or somehow related to the witness. Apparently accounting for the vast majority of all sightings, *familials* are not only the most common type of ghost, but are often seen but once, usually by a grieving spouse or parent—

presumably in an effort to comfort or reassure the bereaved—and never again, thereby making them among the most short-lived variety as well. Unfortunately, this makes them among the most difficult to study as well since no return appearance is usually anticipated, although incidents of *familials* making more than a single appearance is not unheard of.

The second type of interactive personality is the *historical*, which is roughly defined as the manifestation of a person not personally known to the witness but who is still identifiable as a known deceased individual. The ghost of Abraham Lincoln is probably the best known example of a *historical*, though, of course, one need not be famous to become a *historical*; simply being identifiable to the observer is enough. Also, unlike *familials, historicals* are among the more long-term manifestations one might encounter—frequently choosing to haunt a particular locale for years or even decades at a time and being seen by countless witnesses over a considerable period of time—making them especially good study cases. In fact, it could be argued that *historicals* are what make paranormal research even possible, for without their longevity and, to some degree, persistence, ghost hunting would have to remain firmly entrenched within the world of storytelling and anecdotal evidence.

The third type of interactive personality is called the *anonymous*, who is, as one might guess, quite simply the manifestation of a human being whose identity remains unknown to the observer. An example of such a personality might be that of a Revolutionary War soldier who regularly appears in the cellar of a home built on the grounds of an eighteenth-century battlefield, but for whom no record exists by which he might be identified. Since he was never a resident of the locale he is haunting and no historical records capable of placing a name to the apparition exist, this type of entity remains anonymous throughout its existence.

Like the *historical*, an *anonymous* personality is also often a long-term manifestation capable of being studied and, as such, another good subject for research. However, unlike *historicals*, they can be more unpredictable and among the more difficult entities with which to interact, for unlike *historicals* (who usually consider themselves still a part of their environment), the *anonymous* frequently appears to be frightened or confused and sometimes even seems to be as afraid of the living as the living are of them. As such, it tends to be more difficult to get an *anonymous* to "come out and play," and so they do not generally make as good a test subject as do *historicals*, though, of course, there is always the occasional exception.

It should be remembered that while these three subcategories seem to be set, they are, in fact, largely relative and even, to some degree, interchangeable. For example, a *familial* personality may be someone else's *historical* or another person's *anonymous*, depending upon the relationship of the witness to the ghost (or lack thereof), making each type superfluous at best. In the end, it is probably best to refer to all apparently human manifestations that appear capable of interacting within linear time and space simply as personalities and leave it at that.

That being said, however, while these categories may appear on the surface highly subjective, they are, in fact, important. Since skeptics charge that ghostly apparitions are often nothing more than hallucinations induced by the mind-set of the observer, the relationship of the ghost to its observer becomes an important factor in determining the likelihood that a person has had a legitimate paranormal encounter. For example, it is not difficult to understand why a grief-stricken widow might fantasize that she sees the ghost of her dead husband, so the relationship to the observer combined with the observer's mental and emotional state has to be taken into account, especially in the case of *familial* personalities. However, *historicals* (and *anonymous*) personalities are a completely different story. Fantasy- or hallucination-prone individuals, one would assume, would be more likely to conjure up a person they know and are grieving than they would be to manufacture the unexpected and frequently unsettling apparition of a complete stranger. As such, the appearance of a *historical* personality— especially if that apparition appears to multiple, unrelated witnesses over a long period of time—cannot so easily be dismissed. Further, a *historical* entity can be checked against the written record as a form of validation. For example, if three people unknown to each other observe the same ghostly image of a home's prior owner standing at the foot of their bed, and presuming they have no knowledge of the site's history or the fact that it is reputedly haunted, this would constitute strong evidence that a paranormal encounter has taken place. As such, the relationship between the apparition and the observer becomes an important element in determining the likelihood that a manifestation is genuine.

The Noninteractive Personality

The second type of ghostly manifestation is known as the noninteractive personality. Frequently referred to as an *imprint* or *residual energy*, this type of manifestation, while apparently human in appearance and mannerisms, gets its name from the fact that it appears and acts as though it is entirely oblivious to its surroundings. Further, and what specifically differentiates the noninteractive personality ghost with the interactive—aside from this marked lack of awareness of others—is its tendency to repeat the same actions, such as walking down a set of stairs or moving from room to room. Additionally, efforts to communicate with such a manifestation or interact with it in any way are always met by silent indifference, as though it is the observer who is invisible and imperceptible to the ghost rather than the other way around, leading some investigators to question whether such manifestations are disembodied personalities at all or merely a reflection of a moment of time that has somehow been inscribed or imprinted into the environment. In other words, these may not be genuine ghosts at all, but mere pictures or "snapshots" of a once living human going about his or her daily activities that has somehow been recorded by the environment in much the same way a song is imbedded within the swirled indentations of a CD. The biggest problem with this theory, however, is that these manifestations not only frequently appear at different locales throughout a house, but may even appear outdoors.

If we work from the premise that they are mere images engraved upon the environment, however, how do we explain this phenomenon? Even if there might be some process by which human energy is somehow imprinted into the very structure of a building, how might that energy be imprinted upon an open field? For this theory to work, there has to be some medium upon which to imprint the entity in the first place, making these anomalies all the more inexplicable.

More importantly, many in the paranormal community who hold to the imprint theory fail not only to answer the question of what physical process might be involved in imprinting a scene into an environment, but fail to take into account more prosaic possibilities. For example, could such a manifestation be unable to interact or is it simply *choosing* not to interact? For that matter, is it possible it's not even aware it is visible to the still living at all? In other words, could an "imprint" really be nothing more than the manifestation of a personality that lacks the ability to perceive the living and so goes about its business entirely unaware it is being watched? In such a case, then, its tendency to repeat the same actions may be no more remarkable than is our own tendency to repeat precise routines day in and day out in our own world. We often walk through our home via the same route, open and close the same doors in order, sit in the same chairs, gaze out the same windows, all with similar regularity, so there is no reason an earthbound ghost, especially if it were unaware it was visible to the living, might not keep the same routine it maintained in life.

In either case, the noninteractive personality remains the most easily observed of all the ghostly phenomenon as they are sometimes repeatable, usually confined to a particular locality that can be carefully monitored, and, to some degree, even predictable. Whether they are true personalities or mere imprints of human energy, however, remains a source of debate.

The Living Ghost

Perhaps one of the most remarkable types of interactive ghost is not a ghost at all, but the possible projection of a still living person. Known as a "living" ghost and extremely rare, there are a few anecdotal accounts of people encountering manifestations of an individual, usually a good friend or family member, that appear quite spontaneously hundreds or even thousands of miles from their current location. Usually such manifestations, which often have all the earmarks of a ghostly encounter, occur when the subject in question is facing great distress or danger. For instance, a pilot flying through a bad storm might suddenly appear to his family safe and sound hundreds of miles away. It is as though the spirit or soul is in such an agitated state that it actually leaves the body for a short time and goes to a place of safety, only to return again once the danger has passed. If true, this type of manifestation would be more akin to an out-of-body experience (OBE) than a haunting, for the subject in question remains quite alive and is frequently oblivious to the fact that they appeared to their loved ones half a world away. Also if true, this would not be a true ghost in the traditional sense of the word, but simply a manifestation of spiritual energy being made visible through unique and extraordinary circumstances. As such, stories of living ghosts, while intriguing, must remain firmly entrenched within the realm of unprovable, anecdotal stories.

An only slightly more common yet closely related cousin to the living ghost is the "moment of mortality" ghost. This is the phenomenon in which the manifestation of a person suddenly appears to a friend or family member at the precise moment of their death. A woman, for example, might suddenly awaken from a deep sleep to observe her father, whom she knows to be residing in a nearby nursing home, sitting on the foot of her bed. Though surprised, she is even more amazed to see him suddenly vanish before her eyes, filling her with confusion and consternation. Finally persuading herself she has simply had a strange dream, she falls back to sleep only to be awakened a few hours later by a phone call from her mother telling her that her father had passed away during the night (and, the story often goes, at the precise moment of her ghostly encounter).

Technically, such a manifestation is an example of a *familial* personality (as we defined earlier). I only differentiate it because of its proximity to a particular moment of time, a place, and a particular person. Unfortunately, such phenomenon are, again, exceedingly rare, entirely incapable of being substantiated, and so remain of little value to the paranormal investigator. They do, however, strongly suggest that there exists a strong link between loved ones that transcends death and can manifest itself in strange and unexpected ways.

Animal Manifestations

The question of whether an animal might be capable of manifesting remains a source of considerable debate. It is unknown whether animals possess the prerequisite sentience necessary to be considered a conscious personality, so it is hard to understand how their essence might survive death and be capable of manifesting in the physical realm. However, numerous anecdotal accounts and a few examples caught on film suggest otherwise, so we must take this possibility into account as well.

The first thing such accounts force us to consider is whether animals do, despite assumptions to the contrary, possess more consciousness than we imagine. While it is tempting to jump to such a conclusions, there are a couple of other possibilities that present themselves that we should first consider. First, since many people frequently form a very strong bond with their pets, it is not remarkable when manifestations of those pets sometimes enter into the mix. The question, however, is not whether these manifestations are being produced by the conscious, freewill actions of the deceased pet, as it is assumed human-based ghosts are, but if they are produced subconsciously by the viewers themselves—not in the form of grief-induced hallucinations (though this may sometimes be the case) but as a manifestation of their own unconscious energy. In other words, could the human mind be capable of holding the image of the beloved pet so tightly in its subconscious that it is occasionally capable of inadvertently manifesting the animal under ideal conditions?

If so, the apparition in this case would not be the literal spirit of the dead animal, but a type of "memory bubble" produced by the observer's own inherent but unconscious telekinetic energy. In essence, it is the owner's love for the pet that creates the animal's spectral manifestation, not the inherent nature of the animal itself. The fact that the vast majority of animal ghosts are those of beloved family pets (manifestations of regular farm animals and wild animals being far less common) could be an important clue that this might be the case.

However, since apparitions of animals are occasionally caught on film and sometimes appear to people who have no emotional link with the animal, we have to examine the possibility that animals may, in fact, possess a short-term consciousness, at least on a very basic level. If so, it is theorized the animal's consciousness or soul may attach itself to physical places in the same way some human energies apparently do, but being that it lacks the prerequisite sentience to last, it remains only until the basic energy of the creature fades and it eventually winks out of existence. In other words, the animal's consciousness may initially survive physical death for a time before eventually dissipating into nothingness (or, perhaps, being absorbed into some form of greater "animal consciousness"), much like a glowing ember continues to glow for a time after the fire has gone out.

On the other hand, since most animal manifestations are of higher order animals such as dogs, cats, and horses, it is entirely possible that even low levels of consciousness—that state of awareness just below full sentience—might actually be capable of surviving death. The fact that manifestations of more primitive animals such as reptiles, amphibians, insects, and fish are almost unheard of also strongly suggests such a possibility. Of course, this is all purely speculative, but then just where one might draw the line between sentience and non-sentience is not always easily defined. As such, while I personally find it hard to imagine how an animal's consciousness could survive death, the possibility that it might has to at least be considered.

Inanimate Manifestations

As though the various types of interactive and noninteractive human and animal manifestations are not confusing enough, there is the problem that not all ghosts are animate in nature to contend with as well. Inanimate objects such as ships, trains, automobiles, and aircraft, have been regularly reported and remain among the most difficult type of manifestation to account for.

Perhaps the best known of these is the legendary *Flying Dutchman*— an eighteenth-century schooner that allegedly would appear to frightened mariners during the nineteenth century (sometimes as a harbinger of doom)—but more contemporary manifestations are recorded as well: World War I biplanes seen to be flying over long-abandoned airdromes and early racing cars suddenly appearing on modern tracks during qualifying runs. While hoaxing and simple over-imagination could account for some of these stories, many of these tales have been recounted by often reliable witnesses, so it would be premature to dismiss them all out of hand.

The problem is, of course, that since inanimate objects do not possess consciousness and were never alive in any sense of the word, their appearance as a manifestation of energy remains inexplicable. Perhaps one answer is that they are not actual manifestations of physical energy at all, but mirages or prerecorded impressions of some kind, making them more akin to an imprint than a true ghost. The difficulty with this theory, however, is, as we touched upon a moment ago, the lack of environment upon which to imprint the object. A phantom airplane, for example, could hardly have been somehow imprinted upon the currents of air in the same way a person might be imprinted into the building material of a house. Air is not a stable medium like wooden beams or plaster, making such a phenomenon all the more inexplicable. The same is true with ghost ships as well, with the ever-changing sea being a logically unlikely medium upon which to hold and replay the image of a ship.

Another possibility is that since these objects almost always have a pilot or crew, the vessel or vehicle could simply be an appendage of the source entities' manifesting powers. In other words, the ghost that is operating the aircraft or automobile is responsible for creating the apparition, producing it in much the same way it might manifest an apparently physical body from residual energy in the atmosphere (a point we will consider in more detail later). As such, a World War I biplane manifests itself as such only because its pilot either knowingly or inadvertently wills it to do so, thus making the plane a ghostly extension of himself. This, at least, would be one way of getting around several problems the idea of inanimate manifestations produces.

In any case, inanimate manifestations (sometimes also called apparitions) are uncommon and tend to be noninteractive (though not always). They are also usually one-shot affairs that do not repeat themselves, making them difficult subjects to study or document. However, there are a few exceptions: battles fought long ago are reported to sometimes replay themselves under ideal conditions, while the sounds of battle can still occasionally be heard rumbling off the horizon. Whether this is some kind of imprint or an example of something called a time slip (an idea we will examine in more detail later) is unclear, but remains a good area for further study.

The Poltergeist

Probably the most famous type of ghost is the *poltergeist* (German for "noisy ghost"). The poltergeist is best known for its tendency to move (and, in many cases, hurtle) objects across a room, hide small trinkets from the living, and produce a cacophony of noises (usually loud and persistent rapping) designed to bring attention to itself. Though generally harmless, they are also capable of more dangerous stunts such as tripping and slapping and even starting small fires, and though instances of someone being injured by a poltergeist are rare, their ability to frighten people could lead to emotional or health problems in the more fainthearted or injury in people fleeing such entities in panic.

Until recently, poltergeists were thought to be typical personalities—that is, the ghosts of angry or mischievous individuals—but this idea has been recently challenged and, to a large degree, progressively discarded by the paranormal community. Once it was noticed that poltergeist activity normally centered around a single person (usually a young prepubescent girl or some highly sensitive or nervous individual), it was hypothesized that it was not ghosts that were doing the damage, but intense levels of highly charged telekinetic energy the victims themselves were putting out that were responsible for the phenomena. In essence, a stressed youth might be unconsciously moving objects through telekinesis (the ability to move objects with the power of the mind), making them, in effect, both the perpetrator and the victim of a haunting at the same time! This theory not only neatly explains why poltergeist activity abruptly ceases when a certain individual is no longer present, but why it sometimes follows them to other locations as well, and why most activity stops once the individual either reaches adulthood or learns to deal with their anxiety. It also accounts for why poltergeist hauntings rarely produce visual manifestations at haunting sites: there is no actual ghost at all, only unconscious, telekinetic energy, thus making the poltergeist less a type of ghost than a type of telepathic anomaly.

On the surface, this theory seems to be an ironclad explanation for poltergeist activity, but like so much in this field of study, it again fails to account for everything. While ghostly manifestations are rare at poltergeist hauntings, they are not unheard of, and there have even been cases of communication being made with spirit energies at a poltergeist site. In fact, poltergeist activity is often an element of many hauntings, suggesting that at least some of it may be the manifestations of malicious or mischievous spirits rather than all the work of subconscious telekinetic energy. Additionally, it doesn't account for why such a phenomena isn't more common, especially considering how many stressed teenagers there are in the world. It would seem that if nervous energy alone is truly capable of moving objects teleki-netically, high schools should be veritable hot beds of poltergeist activity (especially around the time that finals are being taken).

The other problem with the theory is that it fails to answer the question of why, if some humans seem to possess the ability to move objects with their mind, ghosts shouldn't be similarly capable of doing the same thing. After all, if telekinesis exists in the physical world, it stands to reason it should exist on the "other side" as well (and proba-bly work in much the same way). As such, there is no real rationale why a poltergeist couldn't be the manifestation of a disembodied human personality just as easily as it could be the inadvertent telekinetic energy of a very corporeal person. Obviously, it is an issue that deserves more consideration before a final verdict is rendered.[4]

Nonhuman Manifestations: The "Extra-Celestial"

If we work from the premise that the universe is a very big place, likely home to countless races of intelligent, sentient beings, both physical and potentially noncorporeal in nature, it would be presumptuous to presume that all ghosts are necessarily human. In fact, the ghosts of human beings (personalities) may account for only a tiny fraction of all the spiritual beings in the universe, so another category is needed to differentiate this group from the purely human personality. I pro-pose that "extra-celestials" is an appropriate term for this variety of intelligent energies.

To be more precise, extra-celestials are defined as sentient beings that either once existed as physical creatures on another planet or are entities that have always existed in a noncorporeal state as a being of pure energy. Unlimited by the restrictions of either human mortality or the vagaries of linear time and space, they are the free-roaming and often ancient intellects that may well constitute the majority of all

---

4. Later we will examine other possible explanations for poltergeist activity and the potential link certain people may have with mischievous personalities.

sentient, noncorporeal life that makes up the universe. They may, potentially, even be inter-dimensional beings who naturally reside on another plane of existence far outside of our venue or comprehension, but who occasionally choose to interact with us for some specific reason (most likely having to do with humanity's ongoing quest for spiritual development or even, potentially, its protection, although, of course, this is all purely conjectural).

Extra-celestials are further distinguished from personalities in the markedly different ways in which they interact with the living, at least when compared to human-based ghosts. Whereas personalities tend to do and say very human things, extra-celestials operate on a different level. They are frequently spiritual masters or teachers in the process of dispensing tremendous wisdom or angelic beings willing and able to intervene in human affairs (see chapter thirteen on spirit guides). Additionally, extra-celestials are extremely difficult to document, as they normally interact in more subtle ways than do human-based personalities. For instance, they rarely appear to the naked eye (though some mediums claim to be able to see them) nor are they usually recorded as speaking in audible voices. Instead, they seem to prefer to work behind the scenes, functioning essentially as guides for lost or confused personalities that are still caught in the earth plane, or as overseers of the spiritual realm sent basically to keep order. Further, just as there are malevolent humans to contend with, it is possible there are malevolent extra-celestials as well. Could these entities serve as the foundation for many of the demon mythologies inherent in most religions? It's an intriguing possibility that we will deal with later. In either case, it should be abundantly obvious that the spiritual realm may be a far more complex and, some might say, even crowded arena than we might appreciate. But then, if the universe is as vast a place as we imagine, should we be surprised by anything less?

Conclusion

Having established a basic terminology in our efforts at understanding what a ghost is, it is necessary to ask ourselves the next logical question: just how does a disembodied personality manifest itself? Even more remarkable, how are ghosts able to move physical objects (as they are often reported as doing) if they possess no physical mass? And, finally, why do they sometimes appear to some people but not to others, and, even more maddening, why don't they appear on film when the photographer sees them standing right in front of him and yet often appear on photos without the photographer being aware of their presence? In the next few chapters we will attempt to answer these questions as we deal with the "nuts and bolts" of ghosts, not only on a materialistic level, but on an emotional and personal level as well. In essence, we will be doing nothing less than examining just how a ghost operates, what it's made of, and, most importantly of all, just what it is that makes a ghost "tick."

chapter four

The Mechanics of a Haunting

Just how a disembodied personality might manifest itself in such a way that it can be seen, heard, and even touched by the still living, despite remaining a being with no physical substance, is a question that not only forms the basis for a remarkable mystery, but is the fundamental question all paranormal investigators must deal with when stalking their quarry. It is extremely important that the investigator have some basic ideas of what a ghost is as well, for it is extremely difficult to prove the existence of something when we cannot even begin to guess at what it is made of, how it functions within the physical realm, and what it is trying to do. Without some working theory of what and how ghosts operate, it is akin to trying to put together a jigsaw puzzle with half the pieces missing and no idea of what the final picture is supposed to look like.

Fortunately investigators are not left flailing about in the dark without a clue; there are a number of working theories as to what a ghost is and how it might function within linear time and space. Of course, many of these ideas are unavoidably highly speculative, for no one has actually trapped a ghost to study it under laboratory conditions or, at least as far as I know, talked to one directly about how it manages its feats of physical manifestation. However, that doesn't prevent investigators from coming up with some very interesting ideas about what they think spiritual entities might be and how they operate—ideas we will take a look at here in our quest to understand how such a thing as the human personality might not only survive physical death, but, in fact, be capable of interacting within the physical world without a physical body.

The Hallucination Hypotheses

Before moving on to examine these theories in detail, however, and in an effort to be fair and balanced in our approach, it is first necessary to look at both sides of the equation and examine the skeptic's point of view as well. As such, we will start with the most common answer the debunking community maintains for explaining away ghosts, which is that all such phenomena is nothing more than the product of an overactive imagination or the manifestations of a superstitious and easily suggestible mind.

Since it is a poorly kept secret that ghosts often appear to some people more regularly than others, it has been suggested that, when it comes to ghosts, it is more a matter of believing is seeing rather than the other way around. In other words, it has been suggested that just as there are those people who seem to see UFOs in every night sky and Bigfoot behind every tree, there are those who, either because of a fantasy-prone personality or an incredulous or highly excitable nature, see things the rest of us do not. In essence, people see ghosts because they want to see them (or even need to see them), either to reassure themselves that a deceased loved one is well or to confirm their own assumed immortality. In effect, then, it is not that *seeing* is *believing* in regards to ghosts, but that *believing* is *seeing*.

From a purely scientific/empirical perspective, of course, this makes sense. Since there is no hard evidence that the personality does or even could potentially survive death, all ghosts must be, by the process of elimination—once fraud and mistaken identity have been omitted as possible causes—hallucinations, probably triggered by the trauma of losing a loved one or the fear induced by the thought of one's own mortality.

However, while this theory has many advantages—the most important being its capacity to remove the entire issue from the realm of serious scientific consideration—in the end it creates more problems than it solves. While undoubtedly certain excitable, fearful, or grief-stricken people do imagine things that aren't there, it does not account for those individuals who do not fit into any of these categories but have had a paranormal experience nonetheless. While ghosts sometimes appear to individuals who possess what some refer to as "fantasy prone" personalities, they more often appear to mature, responsible, and sober individuals who had no desire or expectation of seeing one. In fact, the overwhelming majority of people who have encountered a ghost were quite surprised by the experience, irrespective of their beliefs about the afterlife. While people who believe in ghosts do occasionally see one, so do people who either have no strong opinion on the subject or have traditionally held a skeptical view of such a thing. Further, the author himself can attest to the fact that there are many people, among which he includes himself, who are quite open to the idea of encountering a ghost, yet have never seen one. As such, there is simply no evidence to demonstrate that a correlation exists between the need or desire to see a ghost and the incidence of actually seeing one. As such, the hallucination theory is a simplistic and, I think, disingenuous attempt to blithely explain away those things that science is uncomfortable with or unwilling to look at seriously. Simply presuming that everyone who sees a ghost is either looking to see one (or, conversely, is afraid of seeing one) and so inadvertently produces the very hallucination they eventually experience makes for lazy thinking.

Additionally, this explanation assumes that hallucinations are common when, in fact, they are not. True visual or auditory hallucinations among the general population are relatively rare. Outside of those who suffer from certain mental disorders or have used hallucinogenic drugs, the average person is unlikely to experience a genuine hallucination throughout the course of their lifetime. One may occasionally misidentify a strange noise or be tricked by the play of light and shadows across a surface and, of course, we have all experienced naturally occurring mirages, but seeing something that appears quite solid and fully real yet is entirely illusory is exceedingly rare. It happens, but it hardly seems a plausible explanation for the majority of paranormal encounters.

Additionally, the hallucination theory does not explain how ghostly images can be captured on film or inexplicable voices recorded on audiotape, nor can it account for how a hallucination might create a spike in an electromagnetic field or lower the ambient temperature twenty degrees in one corner of a room. In other words, if all ghosts are hallucinations, every piece of physical evidence—every bit of it— must be discounted as fraud, instrument malfunction, or operator error. This would mean omitting a mountain of data in an effort to maintain a particular bias, which, while possibly allowing for an easier and more understandable world, makes for very poor science. While there are those who have expended a sea of ink in maintaining this theory, it does little to help us understand the metaphysical nature of the phenomenon of ghosts. It may be helpful in understanding the nature of the human mind, but it does nothing to help us unravel the mystery before us, and so, beyond reminding us of the ongoing need to take into account the mental and emotional state of all witnesses, it has little to contribute to our investigation.

The Waking Dream Hypothesis

If they are honest, even the most ardent skeptic will admit that some witnesses appear quite levelheaded and matter-of-fact about their experiences, forcing some to allow for the possibility that a witness to a ghostly manifestation may not necessarily be a person in possession of an overactive and overwrought imagination, but may, in fact, have had a genuinely startling and inexplicable experience of coming into the presence of what appears to be a ghost. Of course, they don't believe such a person has had a genuine paranormal experience. Instead, look for their answer elsewhere. Frequently, they find it in their own sub-conscious in the form of a phenomenon known as a hypnagogia.

Better known as a "waking dream," hypnagogia is a type of hallucination that sometimes occurs when a person is just starting to awaken from a sound sleep but has not yet reached the level of complete consciousness. Stuck at some point in the sleep process when the mind is less capable of distinguishing fact from fantasy, the person may mistake dream images as real and decide they have had a paranormal visit. For example, a woman might be dreaming about her recently deceased mother and then awaken to find her standing at the foot of her bed. Since we frequently don't recall our dreams, people might well not realize that the image before them is a product of their unconscious mind and take it for a physical manifestation of their departed love one.

My own grandmother had precisely such an experience that clearly illustrates this point. My biological father died when I was a boy, and, about two months after he passed, my grandmother claims she was lying in bed one morning thinking about the day ahead when the ghostly apparition of my deceased father appeared at her bedroom door. She claimed he looked quite solid and much as he had in life, and he stood watching her with a look of consternation on his face. My grandmother claimed that while surprised, she was not afraid of the unexpected apparition and even had the presence of mind to attempt to dialogue with the specter. Apparently, all she was able to get out of him was a query as to how "the kids" (his six surviving children) were doing, and, upon being assured that they were fine, he simply turned around and walked out of view, never to be seen again.

Initially my grandmother insisted she had not been dreaming and certainly had not been thinking about my deceased father, but pressured by a devoutly Catholic family—which did not handle things like the appearance of a deceased relative particularly well—she later recanted and admitted she had probably just dreamt the whole experience. Whether she truly had or not remains unknown, but it is the sort of experience a waking dream would provide, especially since the apparition of my father not only appeared fully opaque and lifelike, but was able to so effortlessly communicate with her (as opposed to most ghostly encounters).

Hypnagogic dreams as an explanation for mysterious apparitions appearing and interacting with an observer have become especially popular in the wake of an ever-burgeoning number of alien abduction stories. Accounts of quite rational people being taken by "gray men with large black eyes" into an alien spacecraft and medically probed have done much to bolster the skeptic's charge that people don't need to be hallucinating or lying to make an extraordinary claim, but that they need only be dreaming. Additionally, since ghosts often appear to people when they are lying in bed—and who have often just been awoken from a sound sleep by "something" that appears unexpectedly in the room— the case for hypnagogia is made even stronger. As such, the waking dream phenomenon has become a powerful tool in the skeptic's arsenal of explanations, and one that needs to be taken seriously.

As attractive as the waking dream theory might be, however, there are a few problems with it that need to be taken into account as well. For example, hypnagogia does not explain those cases when complete strangers recount having a nearly identical encounter with the same entity months or even years apart, nor does it account for those instances when an entity appears to more than one person at a time. People simply don't share dreams, hypnagogic or otherwise, thus suggesting that something unusual must be taking place. Additionally, what are we to make of those cases in which the ghost is of a historically identifiable individual? It is difficult to explain why a person might dream about a property's long-deceased owner, for example, and then have that person inadvertently appear before them. It just doesn't hold together logically.

Finally, this theory doesn't account for those who see ghosts when they are not in bed, but are going about their business fully awake and aware. It would seem for the hypnagogic model to work, someone would have to be, at a minimum, asleep at the time (or at least in an extremely relaxed state of mind). Unless we are capable of nodding off without even realizing it, it seems hypnagogia as a one-size-fits-all explanation leaves much to be desired.

In the end, the fact that ghosts often appear at night to people who have been awoken from a deep sleep may ultimately have less to do with waking dreams than it does the heightened sensitivity to spiritual energy most people may possess when they are relaxed. Just as we often are not aware of the rhythmic ticking of a clock until we have turned the lights off and are about to drift off, so too may we be better able to perceive the presence of noncorporeal energies around us once we clear our mind of the worries and concerns of the day and really listen. As such, while undoubtedly some ghostly encounters are the result of a waking dream, this would seem to account for a comparatively small percentage of all such experiences, and so a more all-encompassing explanation must be devised to explain away ghostly encounters. Fortunately, just such a theory may be available, and it is one that has the advantage of permitting the dead to be every bit as real as the living.

The Telepathy Theory

Among parapsychologists there exists an increasingly popular belief that ghostly entities may be capable of and more willing to speak to us through telepathy. It has even been suggested that ghosts may actually prefer to communicate in this fashion for a number of reasons, most having to do with issues of practicality. In fact, spiritual entities may have an easier time communicating with us while we are in an unconscious state, such as while in REM sleep or during the in-between state where hypnagogia takes place, and so they may do most of their interworld communication then. In effect, ghosts may be quite able to produce an image of themselves in our mind's eye to use as an aid in communicating with us that our senses simply fall for and mistake for physical reality.

If true, however, this would have some interesting ramifications. For example, it would mean that even an apparent hallucination or a waking dream could still be an authentic attempt at communication from the other side (making the appearance of my deceased father to my grandmother, while not a genuine physical manifestation of disembodied conscious energy, a genuine projection of my deceased father's spirit trying to acquire information from a familial source, thereby making his query about his children a genuine and, apparently, successful attempt at spirit communication). Additionally, it would also neatly explain why some ghosts appear so substantive, even to the point where they can be touched and conversed with, and why they can appear to one person in a group without being seen by others.

This idea may also go far in explaining those especially meaningful and timely dreams we sometimes experience that seem to impact our life in very significant ways. My wife, for example, while considering whether or not she should marry me so soon after coming out of a failed marriage, had a vivid dream in which she had the opportunity to sit down at the kitchen table with her deceased father and discuss the pros and cons of the idea with him (a conversation in which I presume the pros outweighed the cons). While it would be easy to dismiss this incident as a fantasy brought about by her uncertainties or some sentimental desire on her part to acquire her deceased father's blessing, could it not just as easily have been his way of demonstrating he was still involved in her life? I suppose the skeptic would simply assume the former, but it seems presumptuous to imagine that the dead—if indeed their personalities do survive intact—would not make use of such a mechanism to do so. We understand the purpose and functions of dreams so poorly as it is, that they could occasionally (and, some might say, frequently) be genuine communication with the spiritual realm must be considered at least a possibility.

Of course, ghostly telepathy does not account for why ghostly phenomenon is sometimes caught on film or detected by instrumentation, nor does it explain how a ghost could manifest itself telepathically to two or more people at once, yet it does hold some appeal to the paranormal investigator in that it does explain some especially credible encounters for which there exists no corroborating physical evidence, as well as opens another avenue by which a disembodied consciousness might be able to interact with its loved ones without going through the difficult process inherent to physically manifesting. Unfortunately, such a possibility could also have darker implications as well. Telepathy, for example, would go far in explaining the well-documented modern phenomenon of alien abductions as well as its forerunner—attacks upon women by a nighttime apparition known as a succubus that were commonly reported during Victorian times.[5]

However, if ghosts do communicate with us telepathically, it brings up the question of why they don't do so more often and, further, why they don't appear regularly to everyone. After all, we all sleep, we all dream, and we all have lost loved ones we might be desirous of keeping in touch with, so why isn't ghostly communication reported more often than it is?

Several possibilities present themselves, both from the perspective of the ghost as well as from that of the observer. First, some ghosts may simply lack the desire or need to communicate with us, or they may be hesitant to insert themselves into the lives of the still living for various reasons. Additionally, there may be a possibility that there are elements beyond their control that limit their ability to contact the living; it could be, in fact, that it is a capability only the most determined spirits are capable of achieving. In other words, in much the same way that most people lack inherent athletic prowess or musical ability, some entities may simply lack the skills to contact us, even telepathically.

On the other hand, the problem may not lie with them, but with us. It may simply be that most people lack the ability to connect with these entities even in the dream state. Certainly, the idea that there are

---

5. For those unfamiliar with the term, a succubus is essentially a ghostly rapist who assaults women (and, in some rare cases, men as well) in their beds. Obviously, since a ghostly attacker would have no physical body with which to carry out such an assault, it makes one willing to entertain the possibility that it is not the body a malevolent entity is attacking, but the mind. In other words, could a rape take place entirely within the confines of the human psyche, while its effects and the trauma it produces appear every bit as real as if it had literally, physically happened?

some people who are more telepathically sensitive than others and so potentially more capable of seeing and communicating with a ghost does make sense and would have the added advantage of being able to explain professional mediums and psychics (as well as accounting for those instances when one person in a group can perceive a ghostly apparition that everyone else remains oblivious to). Just as some people seem to be more sensitive or perceptive to certain colors, sounds, and odors than most, it might be possible that some people perceive paranormal energy in ways the average person cannot.

The idea that there are people more capable of perceiving spiritual energy than others has been well-documented. I have had a personal experience with just such a person. While a student in art school many years ago I had a classmate who professed an ability to see brightly colored auras around classmates and, while she was a bit eccentric in some ways, she was not crazy. She was quite matter-of-fact about it and found it curious that all people couldn't see auras the way she could. It was as if she were simply able to perceive things others could not (much as dogs can hear sounds humans cannot). Her innate ability seemed quite natural and normal to her, but completely beyond my comprehension (though not my appreciation). As such, it would be foolhardy to disallow the possibility that some people might have a special ability to perceive things to a degree the average person cannot.

Finally, it is possible that most people do receive telepathic communications from the dead all the time, but it comes to them in such a way that they are unable to recognize it as such. For instance, a deceased parent might telepathically communicate to a child that they are in danger in such a way that the child, while sensing a certain uneasiness about an impending activity (such as, say, skydiving), doesn't interpret it as a message from the dead parent. To them, it appears as a hunch or a sense of foreboding, which they will hopefully seriously consider and act on. The fact is, we simply don't know what methods the departed may have to keep in touch with us, so it may be wise to pay particularly close attention to our hunches and intuition in the future, for they could be attempts by the other side to warn us of dangers or difficulties in this life.

The Time Slip Theory

Before moving on to other, more materialistic theories about how ghosts operate, it is first necessary to briefly explore one more idea about how and why they appear that has gained some adherents within the paranormal community. That is the idea that ghosts are not really manifestations of energy or even telepathic communicators, but simply people who have somehow stepped outside of time.

This theory works from the premise that time is fluid rather than fixed. In other words, time is not truly linear as we experience it, but exists within the context of a single point of space. If true, it would not be impossible to imagine that a person might somehow "slip" from one point in time to another in much the same way a person might move from one room to another within their home. As such, the image of an apparently very solid personality moving through a mansion completely oblivious to the presence of the observer may not be a ghostly encounter, but a snapshot from an earlier time that has somehow invaded the viewer's own time frame.

Such an explanation would do much to explain those ghosts, commonly known as imprints or residual manifestations, who appear entirely oblivious to the observer and treat them as though they are invisible. Are they really just unaware of the observer, or are they oblivious to our world not because they are dead, but because they have somehow stepped out of time?

How this might work, of course, is completely unknown. However, it could account for a small percentage of incidents in which apparently sober and rational people have reported finding themselves in decidedly ancient surroundings—sometimes for minutes or even hours at a time—as though they had just stepped out of a time machine.[6] Might it not also account for those apparitions that occasionally appear to us dressed in period costume, apparently completely unaware of our presence?

While an intriguing hypothesis and an interesting idea to file away in the back of our mind, the time slip hypothesis is probably not as useful in explaining ghosts as are other theories. It is simply too complex and riddled with unknowns to be helpful. Except as a possible explanation for the few reported cases of vintage aircraft or recreations of ancient battles that witnesses have periodically reported, it would seem to have little to offer in terms of understanding ghostly phenomena. I offer it as only one idea of many currently in vogue, but one that does offer some interesting possibilities.

The Ghost as Energy Theory

Probably the most prevalent and accepted theory about what ghosts are, at least among those who study this phenomenon in some detail, is that they are a collection of energy that has somehow found a means of manifesting itself within the physical realm. In effect, ghosts are simply collections of naturally occurring, ambient energy that possesses the ability to interact within the world of linear time and space.

While from a purely scientific standpoint this seems most fantastic, the idea is not nearly so remarkable once we recognize that everything (including ourselves) is actually made up of particles of energy in the form of atoms that appear, at least from our perspective, as solid matter. Yet there is nothing about us that is "solid" in the truest sense of the word, for as we discussed earlier, the atoms that make up our physical bodies are composed largely of empty space, making our apparent solidity really only an illusion. A ghost, then, may be nothing more than what we are, only on a greatly diminished level. In effect, ghosts may be nothing more than people who possess the ability to

---

6. Colin Wilson records several accounts of such a phenomenon in his book *Beyond the Occult* (Carroll & Graf Publishers, 1989).

attract enough energy to become solid enough to be seen, though not solid enough to become flesh and blood, making them, at least in that respect, truly nothing more than shadows of their former selves.

The most common theory as to how this mechanism might work is that a disembodied cloud of intelligent energy—the remnants of a once physical mind that is determined to manifest itself—pulls ionized atoms from the atmosphere and begins to bring them together in such a way and in sufficient quantities that, under ideal conditions, it accumulates enough mass to reflect light or be detectable to sensitive equipment (or be perceived by people predisposed to perceiving such energy).

But is such an idea even potentially feasible? That the atmosphere is filled with static electricity is a well-established fact of physics. This can be clearly demonstrated by simply shuffling one's feet across a newly installed carpet and touching a metal fixture. For the most part, such energy is harmless, and, though it can be dangerous (a static electric discharge may have been responsible for the explosion that destroyed the hydrogen-filled airship *Hindenburg* in 1937), it is generally useless unless one wishes to annoy one's friends by shocking them with static discharges. Further, ionized atoms, the byproduct of an electrically unbalanced atom, exist all around us and, in sufficient quantities, can form something called plasma (the most common but probably least understood fourth state of matter), which has proven itself to be a highly usable form of energy. Ghosts have even been known to pull power from batteries at a haunting, apparently in an attempt to acquire enough charged atoms to, if not appear, at least move objects. As such, the idea that the environment itself may be a major factor in determining the possibility that a ghost might appear has to be considered a very real one and may have more to do with the success or failure of acquiring evidence of the paranormal than we might imagine.

Yet even if all of this is true, how might a ghost be able to make use of such energy? What mechanism could permit a disembodied personality to create something like plasma or, at a minimum, accumulate enough energy to create an electromagnetic signature or produce an image on a film negative?

Through the sheer energy of thought itself.

The Creative Power of the Mind

Everything that the human mind has conceived and built exists on this planet as a byproduct of thought. Every invention, every man-made object, every structure, every painting, and every book first started out as an idea in someone's mind that was eventually given form and, ultimately, existence. As such, since nothing exists that was created by the hand of man that did not first originate in the mind, it stands to reason that the mind is a powerful and ongoing tool of creation. As such, it follows that if the mind survives the death of the body, it should still retain those formidable powers of creation and so be capable of producing things through the sheer power of its intellect alone (just as it frequently did in life).

Of course, there is a big difference between producing something with our hands and manufacturing plasma from ambient energy, but perhaps it only appears that way from our limited perspective; after all, anything we might build and plasma are made out of the same "stuff" (particles of energy in the form of atoms), so the thought that one is any more difficult to produce than the other is purely a subjective limitation. It may just be a matter of degree; just as people produce or manipulate objects in the natural realm in an effort to bring the creations of their mind into solid form, so might we speculate that the disembodied personality might make similar use of the materials it has access to—ambient energy—in an effort to bring itself into physical manifestation as well. As such, a ghost could well be little more (or less, for that matter) than an attempt by a disembodied mind to pull together the necessary elements required to manifest itself within the physical realm through the *power of its own will*. In other words, a disembodied personality appears to us in ghostly form because it has willed itself to do so, with the power contained within its own consciousness being the mechanism that makes the manifestation possible. It has simply to think that it wishes to appear and, presuming it has mastered the abilities required to do so and the environmental conditions are right, it will collect the necessary ambient energy from the atmosphere until it has acquired sufficient density to take on visible form. This would not only give it the ability to appear when and where it wanted, but would explain why ghosts sometimes appear in complete human form (and are usually fully clothed at that) and why they frequently look as they appeared in life at a particular age. Certainly a disembodied personality should have no need for such considerations in its natural state, implying that such detail, then, is a product of the imagination—not of the viewer, *but of the ghost itself!*

Of course, this brings up the question of why ghosts aren't more common if it's all simply a matter of "thinking" themselves into form. There are a couple of reasons for this. First, as I have already suggested, a disembodied consciousness may be severely limited in its ability to manifest by various physical or environmental factors such as the available amounts of energy in a given location, temperature, humidity, and other meteorological and atmospheric considerations. In fact, investigators frequently note that ghosts tend to appear more often in cooler, damper environments than in warm, dry locales (and more often in winter rather than summer months[7]), implying that there may be times when available energy sources are more conducive toward manifestation than at other times. As such, a partial manifestation may simply be the result of poor atmospherics or a lack of enough ionized energy to "get the job done."[8]

Even if the conditions are ideal for manifesting, however, the second reason an entity may have trouble doing so may lie within itself. Since the individual personality probably possesses only a certain level of awareness, it may not realize the tremendous power available to it, and so it inadvertently limits its own ability to manifest. In essence, it

---

7. Joshua Warren, *How to Hunt Ghosts*, (Simon & Schuster, 2003), page 590.

8. This does suggests the exciting possibility, however, that one might be able to help a ghost manifest by providing a plentiful energy source for it to make use of, such as a generator.

can only do that which it believes it is capable of doing. This would explain why some ghosts appear only as filmy vortexes or incomplete bodily manifestations while others appear quite solid and, on occasion, fully interactive; each are simply reflecting their own level of understanding and manifestation talent. In effect, some ghosts are still learning how to use available energy and are not yet skilled enough to make a go of it, while others may have the process down pat.

But this does not answer the question of why a ghost would choose to manifest itself in the first place. Do they do it out of curiosity or mischievousness, or could there be other more problematic reasons to do so? Could it be, for instance, that at least some ghosts are manifestations of lesser evolved energies that are trapped on the earth plane due to some unfinished business or strong attachments to the physical realm, and their efforts at manifesting are their only means of interacting with a world they no longer belong to? Understanding how and why a person might become a ghost could be just as interesting an avenue to explore as understanding how they might manifest, and one we will look at in the next chapter.

One final element to consider before moving on is how a ghost, assuming it is made up of electrical energy being manipulated by the mind of the personality it is manifesting, is capable of doing things like speaking in an audible voice, manufacturing certain odors, and even touching a person. People have reported not only unknowingly speaking with and shaking a ghost's hand as if it were completely physical, but of even being physically assaulted by a ghostly entity! Clearly, this would seem to be something that goes well beyond the ability of mere ionized energy to do. So how do we explain this?

Of course, we could ask the same question of ourselves as well. How do we in the physical realm have the ability to speak, touch, and hold objects if we are composed primarily of fast-moving patterns of energy existing within an ocean of empty space? Obviously, it is a matter of degree. Living in the physical realm as we do, we exist in a world in which the vibrational frequencies of all matter are likely much lower than that of the spiritual realm. Therefore, for a spiritual entity to manifest itself in our world, it would need to lower the frequency at which it operates in an effort to collect enough ambient energy to do things on a physical level. What the entity wants to do, then, will determine how low it needs to reduce its harmonic frequency. If all it wishes to do is appear on film, for example, it may not need to go all that low; staying at the higher levels of the ultraviolet range may be sufficient for its purposes. If it wants to move objects, however, it may need to lower its frequency considerably in an effort to collect the prerequisite energy it requires. However, no matter how far it lowers its frequency, it will never be able to move all the way down to the level where it may become completely solid. Some ghosts might get close and a few might even be skilled enough to appear, on the surface at least, solid enough to interact with the physical realm for a short time, but likely the amount of psychic energy required to hold such a form for more than a few minutes might be more than even the most determined ghost is capable of maintaining. In essence, even the most solid interactive ghost will never be more than a facsimile of its former physical self; an ionized outer shell temporarily held together by nothing more than the sheer force of its own will. Yet that still might be enough to take on form and even produce sounds under the proper circumstances, which is why ghosts often appear far more substantial than logic would seem to allow.

Perceiving the Spiritual Realm through Artificial Means

Before leaving the subject of how ghosts might be perceivable to our senses, we need to briefly touch upon one last aspect of the equation, and that is whether it might be possible to perceive ghosts—or any spiritual entity, for that matter—from our world of the flesh. In other words, is there a way we might peek into the ghostly realm, or is it a one-way journey with only the spirits possessing the power to traverse between the two realms of existence? There are clues that suggest perceiving the spiritual realm may, indeed, be possible, but the price of doing so may be prohibitive.

Stories of individuals committing heinous crimes in response to the instructions of a "voice inside their head" are legion and need to be considered from more than simply a purely psychological perspective. Could there be an external element to these "voices" as well—one that science is unwilling to consider? In such a case, then, it could be that people who recount hearing voices telling them to do evil things are not simply hallucinating, but are, in fact, receiving signals the rest of us cannot pick up. As such, is it possible that some psychosis and other mental disorders might not be entirely hallucinogenic at all, but evidence of brains that are a little too sensitive to the energies produced by the spiritual realm? For a person already prone toward violence, then, a malevolent entity might be able to pick up on those whose "receivers" are tuned to their frequency and flood their senses to the point of insanity.

What I am suggesting here, while hardly original, is highly controversial. I am simply asking whether those people we institutionalize as dangerous psychotics and schizophrenic personalities might be suffering not from delusions but from a heightened sensitivity to other dimensions of reality? In effect, might they simply be people whose brains are wired in such a way that they are able to see into a realm of existence the rest of us cannot but lack the comprehension to make sense of what they see and so hide within a veneer of insanity?

Of course, science points to the fact that many of the symptoms of psychosis can be mimicked in people who are not psychotic themselves through the use of various hallucinogenic drugs, such as LSD and PCP, thus suggesting that such delusions are internally generated by a brain on overload. Laboratory studies and anecdotal stories have shown these powerful drugs to be able to induce many of the classic symptoms of psychosis, up to the point where people report "seeing" mysterious creatures and even hearing voices, making a good case that such images and perceptions are entirely hallucinatory and a result of a scrambling of the brain's neurons.

What clinical psychologists rarely ask, however, is whether hallucinogenics may not simply be a short-term and artificial means of acquiring the same heightened perceptions psychotics and others are able to achieve naturally. In other words, is it possible that hallucinogenics are doing far more than merely manufacturing illusions that the senses are fooled into perceiving to be real? Could they, instead be a means of expanding the brain's ability to see things that exist outside the context of our normal senses—a means of "fine tuning" our built-in spiritual senses beyond their natural limits, allowing us to see into the spiritual realm on a deeper level? LSD has been called a "mind expanding" drug ever since it first appeared. Could that reputation be more precise than we imagine?

Of course, few scientists would accept such an idea because most refuse to entertain the idea that there is or even *could be* a reality that exists outside our ability to perceive it. Yet what if there is a spiritual realm that exists parallel to our own as I have suggested? Wouldn't it make sense that by wiring our brain differently through the use of powerful drugs—in effect, mimicking the way a psychotic's brain is wired—we too might be able to perceive this "other" world, at least to some extent?

There is one problem, however: New Age beliefs teach us that the spiritual realm is a place of peace and love, peopled by entities of light and wisdom. As such, if we were able to "expand" our senses to the point of being able to perceive this world, it should afford the viewer a wonderful experience. Unfortunately, it seems that such is rarely the case, especially among psychotics and many drug users, who often report this other world to be, a frightening and unsettling place populated by strange and bizarre creatures that defy description. So how do we reconcile two such contradictory perspectives? Is the spirit realm a place of light and love as so many mystics (and NDE survivors) affirm, or could they have gotten it wrong after all?

Or could it all be simply a matter of perspective? Perhaps this discrepancy can be explained by our own inability to comprehend such a world. In other words, could the reason many find the spiritual realm so unsettling be not because they are peering into a naturally frightening place but, being that we are creatures used to interacting within the physical realm, because it is so different from anything we are able to understand and comprehend?

If we naturally assume that this physical world is all that exists in the universe, the ability to perceive anything beyond this world must, naturally, prove both strange and frightening. This is why psychotics are so frequently terrified by the things they imagine themselves to be seeing; the images may simply be outside his or her frame of reference and, since we tend to be frightened by what we do not understand, fear is the natural result. It would be the equivalent of a small child being terrified by a roomful of strangers; the strangers may actually be kind and compassionate people, but to the child's undeveloped senses they may appear frightening and threatening.

However, there is another point to consider as well. Our antidrug culture has a natural bias against the use of hallucinogenic drugs, and so we frequently are only told of the most negative "trips" drug abusers experience, while neutral or even positive experiences receive little or no attention. The reason for this is obvious: society does not want people experimenting with such powerful and dangerous drugs, especially for merely recreational purposes, making it imperative that positive results be suppressed or, at best, de-emphasized. Yet such drug gurus as the late Dr. Timothy Leary were enthusiastic proponents of the use of certain hallucinogenics (taken under tightly controlled conditions) and frequently extolled their virtues as a means of "expanding" one's consciousness to new heights of awareness, implying that, for him and others like him, their use of LSD was a positive experience. Perhaps he merely demonstrated that for people who know how to use such drugs safely and who, at the same time, maintain a belief and expectation of a spiritual realm existing alongside our own, such "trips" can frequently be enlightening and even enjoyable. It's interesting to note that most drug users tend to be very young and use hallucinogenics out of curiosity or as a means of escaping reality. Lacking the maturity to anticipate or handle what they might encounter, then, would make them especially likely to be frightened by what they see.[9] As such, maturity and attitude may be prerequisites for having "good trips" as much as immaturity and fear seem to be prerequisites for experiencing a "bad" one.

However, even if such drugs do give one the ability to perceive another dimension, that doesn't mean human beings should try to do so. Most of us (and, probably, the vast majority of us) are neither spiritually nor emotionally evolved enough to handle such an experience. Our brains are specifically designed to operate in this realm of existence; rewiring it to perceive the spiritual realm may do irreparable damage and, in some cases, may even lead to death. Just as one can badly damage or even destroy an electronic device by wiring it differently than it was engineered, so too might one damage the physical brain in the process of rewiring it to perceive that which it was never designed to perceive. In that, then, I believe Dr. Leary and those who agree with his philosophy and enthusiastically endorse the use of hallucinogenics were and are playing a dangerous game. In most cases, the potential risks far outweigh any potential spiritual insights a person might gain from their use and could, in the end, do irreparable damage to the brain itself. One day we may be ready to go to that world, but when and if we do it will be a natural part of our spiritual, intellectual, and emotional evolution and not the result of chemical imbalances or hallucinogenic drugs being put into our systems. There is a reason we cannot easily peer into the spiritual realm and we should honor that.

Conclusion

Whether ghosts use the dream state to communicate with the still living or are able to manifest a body of pure plasma by utilizing the power of the mind and the ambient energy of the atmosphere is likely

---

9. It is also important to note that many drug users report seeing scenes of great beauty and possessing a sense of oneness with the universe as well, which would both be consistent with what one would expect of the spiritual realm and account for why having such experiences have proven so popular.

to remain a source of considerable debate. Most likely, the answer lies in a combination of theories, with some ghosts preferring to manifest one way and others another. Just as we all have different ways we like to organize things, so too may different personalities use various methods to make themselves known. In fact, I would find it both remarkable and somewhat suspicious if all ghosts operated the same way, for it is our uniquely different ways of looking at things and the distinct manner in which we prefer to do things that are the mark of sentience. Individuality and uniqueness are the signs of a human being; ghosts, in continually showing us that they are anything but identical, demonstrate that not only are they very human indeed, but that their personality continues to operate independent of the body that once housed it.

chapter five

The Psychology of Ghosts

Aside from understanding the mechanics of how a ghost might manifest itself in our physical world, an even more interesting question is why one would want to do so in the first place.

If the basic personality does manage to survive the death of the physical body that houses it, it would seem to open an entirely new world for the disembodied and, some might say, unencumbered intellect to explore. If near-death and out-of-body experiences are any indication, they tell us that release from the physical body can be a joyous and fascinating experience, making the rationale behind why one would wish to stay on the Earth plane as a ghost all the more inexplicable. In essence, why play in the physical realm when, by all accounts, the spiritual realm offers so much more?

In this chapter, we will examine some of the more common reasons paranormal investigators give to explain why some souls seem to prefer to stay earthbound while others appear to move on effortlessly. As such, this section will, in many ways, have far more to do with psychology than parapsychology as we examine the ghostly psyche and see if we can figure out what might make a person decide to haunt his old neighborhood when he could well be doing more interesting things.

While at first glance this attempt at understanding the ghostly psyche would appear to be beyond our ability to hypothesize, I disagree. A ghost is only human after all, and we do know a few things about human behavior that we might transpose onto our ethereal associates in an attempt to better understand them. In effect, ghostly behavior shouldn't be all that different from normal human behavior, even if the consciousness that powers it exists within another context of reality.

For the purpose of this study, I'm working from the premise that the personality not only survives physical death, but that it remains conscious, aware, capable of perceiving and interacting with the physical realm (at least to some extent), and is, to a large degree, still capable of making freewill decisions. (How capable it is of perceiving the world it has just vacated and to what degree it would want to or be capable of interacting with it must remain, of course, largely speculative, though we might be able to venture some good guesses.) Only in this way can we possess the means by which we might understand the question of whether anyone can become a ghost or whether it is something that happens to only a select few. This, of course, will force us to consider whether we might not be a good candidate for becoming a ghost ourselves, and, if so, what steps we might take now in an effort to avoid that fate (assuming one considers becoming a ghost to be a bad thing). In any case, it should at least afford us an opportunity to better understand our colleagues on the other side, and, in so doing, perhaps make it easier to communicate with them and, potentially, even help them find their way home.

Ghost By Choice or By Accident?

Perhaps the first thing we need to determine is what factors go into deciding whether a particular person is likely to become a ghost. Does becoming a ghost happen to everyone when they die or only to some? Is it something we choose to do, or can we be accidentally trapped on the Earth plane and be impelled to roam the world of the living for all eternity?

Obviously, we cannot know the answers to these questions with anything approaching certainty, but there are some guidelines we might follow. The first thing to understand about a ghost, and I'm limiting the discussion here purely to those entities we have previously identified as *personalities* (human-based ghosts), is that where human beings are concerned, not even death changes things all that much. I believe that when a person dies they move onto the next realm with all the personality traits, quirks, prejudices, biases, and a lifetime of accumulated wisdom (and nonsense) fully intact and still in operation. That is not to say they cannot learn—and quickly—and so shed some of the more preposterous ideas they drug with them over to the other side (I imagine ardent materialists would have an especially difficult time accepting that they are still conscious, for instance). But, for the most part, we can assume any dramatic changes wrought by one's earthly demise are not going to become immediately apparent in the spirit realm, at least for some time. Working from that premise, then, it is not difficult to imagine how some people would either choose to be a ghost—perhaps out of curiosity or a mischievous bent—or might allow themselves to be trapped on the physical plane by their own personality flaws. As such, we might conclude that the reasons for becoming a ghost may be as numerous and varied as are the types of personalities humans exhibit. Let's look at just a few of the more prevalent ghostly "personality types" and explore their possible rationale for choosing to remain in the physical realm.

The Unaware Ghost

Many paranormal investigators believe that some entities remain within the physical realm simply because they are unaware that they are dead, and so go on about their life much as they did before, completely oblivious to the fact that they are no longer a part of the physical realm. This idea has been popularized by such excellent movies as *The Sixth Sense* and *The Others* and is a part of many people's beliefs about ghosts (another perception Hollywood has done much to reinforce).

I, however, find it extremely unlikely that a person would not recognize that they are dead. Near death experience (NDE) accounts remain remarkably consistent in their insistence that even upon sudden and unexpected death the soul invariably detaches from the body and hovers about nearby, all the while aware of its surroundings and cognizant of the fact that it is no longer attached to its physical body. If these accounts are accurate portrayals of what the human psyche experiences at the moment of death, it seems that to miss the fact that one had "passed over" would be about as hard to miss as would be the loss of a limb; some things, it seems, are just a little too obvious not to notice. Unless one died in their sleep or was so inebriated when they passed, I should imagine the one thing we could not help but notice is our own death, especially once we started encountering deceased loved ones and other spiritual entities (and, perhaps, even various religious figures). As such, I seriously doubt that any recently deceased spirit could be in (or, at least, remain in) such a state of ignorance for long. It simply doesn't hold together logically.

That being said, however, it is possible that children or the mentally handicapped might not recognize the situation for what it is and remain attached to the physical plane after their death. Ghosts of children are frequent subjects of a haunting, leading to the possibility that children who are unable to comprehend death in practical terms may well be too confused to move on after their demise. Death is, after all, generally considered a grown-up affair that is rarely discussed with children.[10] As such, some children may have no real understanding of what is happening to them and so remain trapped in a type of "sleep state" until they either can finally comprehend what has happened and move on or are rescued by other spiritual entities whose job it is to look out for these gentle souls and guide them along.

Such an entity would be more akin to an immature or childish ghost than to an unaware ghost, though, of course, such distinctions are probably more a matter of semantics. For the most part, it is probably safe to assume that most humans will recognize when they are dead and leave it at that.

---

10. Terminally ill children who have had a chance to discuss death, however, often show a remarkable resiliency and acceptance of their own mortality, often far beyond that of many adults. Parents, however, generally attempt to shield their children from such unpleasant subjects and so few healthy children have a real grasp of what death is or a chance to process it, potentially creating great difficulty in adjusting to the afterlife if their death is unexpected or sudden.

The Denial Ghost

While it is unlikely that mature and psychologically stable person would be unaware that they have died, it is entirely possible there are those who find the idea so traumatic that they refuse to accept the fact and live on in utter denial of their new reality.

While at first thought this idea may sound preposterous, when one considers that just as there are people who make denial a major part of their life, it is only natural to imagine that there are those personalities who will make it an integral part of their death as well. Denial, after all, seems to be such a big part of what it is to be a human in the first place that I can't imagine it wouldn't remain a big part of some people's identity after death as well, at least in some cases.

Of course, denying one's death may sound very similar to being unaware of it, but there is a big difference. The unaware ghost allegedly does not realize it is dead whereas even the most obstinate denial ghost knows, at least on some level, that it is dead and is simply refusing to acknowledge the fact. After all, that is the whole point of denial; it is only necessary when one is aware that there is a truth that needs to be suppressed.

To that end, then, some personalities may simply choose to go on as if nothing has happened and ignore every obvious sign that they no longer exist within a physical context in the process. This is possibly what happens to many historical personalities who refuse to vacate a particular location; they will not leave because they can't bear the idea they might be dead, and so they remain, going about their day-to-day affairs as if nothing has changed. They are like the elderly Hollywood starlet who bemoans the lack of privacy her fame has brought long after her name has been forgotten, and refuses to open the door because a part of her knows the adoring throngs of fans she so disdains will not be there. As such, they can be the ones who remain earthbound the longest, for human pride can be as powerful and dehabilitating on the other side as it often proves to be on this side of eternity.

The Attached Ghost

Though in many ways similar to the denial ghost, this type of ghost knows and even fully acknowledges that it is dead, but is so emotionally attached to the things of the world that it refuses to let go of them. Usually they are attached to such things as their home or some place they truly loved, resulting in their energy being too enmeshed within the physical realm—their emotions and perceptions remaining too "earth heavy"—for them to move on, and so they stay behind, always hovering on the edge of human perception but rarely, if ever, able to interact with it in any meaningful way. To many of these entities, then, death is seen simply as a tremendous impediment in their enjoyment of life and one they do their best to ignore or work around.

If their attachment to the things of the world is strong enough, such ghosts can remain around for years or even decades; even if they can no longer enjoy the things they once owned or be able to interact with them, it is still better, from their perspective, than not having them at all. As such, they tend to be possessive entities who insist that new residents leave their home or attempt to interfere in the lives of those they left behind, sometimes in rather significant ways. If strong-willed enough, such entities may stay a very long time, usually not leaving until either their home has been bulldozed or has been so dramatically altered as to make it unlivable to them. (Could this is the reason home renovations frequently induce increased levels of paranormal activity?) Only then may such ghosts finally begin to fade and dissipate, though it may be some time before they will be willing to concede the futility of remaining behind and move on entirely.

As such, people of a possessive or sentimental nature who are extremely attached to their possessions or who are otherwise incapable of functioning outside of the familiar walls of the world they have created for themselves are good subjects for becoming an attached ghost. Overidentification with one's profession or trade can also produce this effect (ghosts of librarians or school janitors, for instance, are examples of this), and elderly couples and shut-ins who have learned to isolate themselves from the outside world especially run this risk and so need to consider the potential repercussions their self-imposed exile may have in the next world. It is never helpful to attach great importance to anything in the physical realm, for it is a temporary environment that is constantly in a state of flux and beyond anyone's ability to control; attached ghosts are simply those individuals who have yet to realize that fact.

The Jealous Ghost

Though exceedingly rare, there are accounts of ghostly entities attaching themselves not to things but to people and interjecting themselves into earthly relationships, usually out of jealousy or spite. This could be anything from an overly possessive spouse who cannot accept the thought of their mate remarrying to a spurned lover who took his or her own life only to come back and attach themselves to the source of their unrequited affections later. Usually active only around the source of their possessiveness and then only when in the presence of that source's newfound affections (when it can produce all sorts of mischief designed to drive the suitor away), the jealous ghost can be among the most difficult, irritating, and hard to get along with entity of all.

However, while this type of ghost is very similar to the attached ghost in that it refuses to break its earthly links because of something in the physical realm it has overidentified with, its source of attention is so limited and fixed that it can usually be gotten rid of fairly easily. Once the still living partner remarries (or otherwise makes it clear to the interfering entity that they intend to get on with their life), it will usually dissipate and move on to other pursuits (though not without usually loitering for a while longer just in case the source of their affection changes their mind).

In most cases, however, it is only the death of its partner that finally ends the haunting, meaning that if it is obstinate enough, a jealous ghost could end up hanging around for decades (though this would be unusual). As such, overly jealous, possessive, or controlling individuals need to be especially careful they don't end up stuck on the physical plane after they die because of their stubborn unwillingness to give up that which they do not truly own in any case. It takes very little, it seems, to stay attached to the temporal realm, so one would be wise to do some introspection where relationships are concerned to see if they may be a good candidate to become a jealous ghost, and, if so, what changes they might need to make in their life to avoid that fate.

The Fearful Ghost

Due to cultural or religious conditioning, some personalities are simply too afraid to find out what fate has in store for them and so prefer the mundane existence of a haunting to the potential punishment a final judgment might portend. Often these are individuals who did considerable harm—or believe they did—to others and so fear being called out for their offenses and punished. To them, then, remaining within the comparative safety of the physical realm is their only means of avoiding the very judgment and punishment they believe they so richly deserve, and so they cling to the material world the way a frightened child might cling to its mother's leg on the first day of school.

It is not just evildoers who find themselves in this state, however, but ordinary people who have been subjected to various fundamentalist religious teachings from childhood (teachings they are certain they have failed to live up to) and so retain a fear of being eternally punished for "backsliding" or for committing some other real or imagined transgression (making them, in effect, ghosts who are doing nothing less than attempting to hide from hell). Guilt and shame can be powerful fear inducers for some people, especially among those who have grown up in a background of religious intolerance or maintained firmly held beliefs in such things as divine wrath, original sin, eternal retribution, and the reality of hell. As such, then, people who have had strong religious beliefs drilled into them from childhood and feel they have not lived up to them are good candidates to become fearful ghosts, especially if they believe God is angry with them and they have not had a chance to repent or otherwise have their sins absolved before they died. Fear is almost as strong an emotion as love and can keep one tied to the Earth plane as completely as denial, possessiveness, and jealousy can.

Of course, there really are nasty people out there who have done some pretty terrible things (we will explore the issue of what might happen to a wicked ghost later), but for now it is enough to recognize that quite often we are our own worst enemy and are usually more adroit at inadvertently torturing ourselves than any external foe (or deity) could ever be.

The Melancholy or Sad Ghost

The fact that some people are so overwhelmed by grief to the point of incapacitation is a sad reminder of the power of unresolved loss to hold a human soul in limbo long after the body that housed that soul has died. As such, we should not be surprised when this type of negative energy manages to manifest itself within our physical realm in the form of the sad or melancholy ghost.

Perhaps the most depressing type of entity one can encounter, the melancholy ghost is one that is so overwhelmed by some tragedy that it continues to wander the physical realm as if in a state of shock from which it seems incapable of recovering. This is why suicides often end up as sad ghosts, for the same factors that drove a person to take their life frequently keep them bound to the very physical realm they took such pains to rid themselves of. Additionally, such entities can also be among the most difficult to rescue, for they are often too self-absorbed in their own pain to either recognize the need for salvation or care about it. They truly are the most lost of all souls and may require significant intervention on both the part of the living and other spiritual entities to pull them toward the light.

Melancholy ghosts often announce their presence by filling a room with an air of sadness or despair that can dramatically impact the still living in often profound ways. They may also be the source of many cemetery hauntings, for in their grief at the loss of their life, they may be drawn to the physical remains of what had once been their only earthly source of joy. In essence, a sad ghost may be drawn to the physical remains of themselves or a loved one in the same way a grieving mother is unwilling to leave the casket of her child. These ghosts simply cannot let go of their loss long enough to notice their own unfortunate state and so remain walking a never-ending treadmill of pain, regret, and despair.

As such, people who suffer from chronic depression or are suicidal need to be aware that they could be setting themselves up to be an earthbound spirit, as could people who have made another person (usually a spouse or a child) so much the centerpiece of their existence that their loss would permanently cripple them emotionally. That is not to say that grief itself could result in a person becoming a ghost, but the inability to come to terms with it that could do the trick. Severe, unprocessed emotions may be the hallmark of an earthbound spirit more often than we might imagine.

The Mission Ghost

A generally more upbeat and even lively entity, this type of ghost stays around in order to take care of some unfinished business that was cut short by their unexpected death. This mission can be as simple as revealing the location of a hidden will or as major as trying to find justice for a life cut short by murder, but in either case mission ghosts seem intent upon achieving some goal they have set for themselves and feel they cannot rest until they have succeeded. (A good example of a mission ghost was the one played by actor Patrick Swayze in the 1990 movie *Ghost.*) As such, they will often be among the most persistent and frequently appearing type of manifestation, for they have important things to do. On the flip side, they are generally also a short-term entity, interacting within the physical realm only long enough to accomplish their goal, after which they abruptly move on.

A unique type of mission ghost is known as the legacy ghost. This is a personality that stays not to accomplish some specific task but to continue to interact with the physical realm as an outlet for its creativity. The case of Mrs. Rosemary Brown of England is a classic example of this sort of manifestation. In 1964 this widow and untutored musician who possessed only the most basic knowledge of the piano began composing sophisticated works she claimed were dictated to her by the spirits of Liszt, Chopin, and Beethoven (among others). Over a period of almost ten years she wrote a number of unique and never-before-heard symphonies of tremendous complexity and professionalism in the styles of various famous musicians, pieces that were largely beyond her own ability to play and that were identified by several professional musicians as consistent with the styles of these great composers. Though there were critics who also contended the pieces to be something less than these composers' best stuff, the fact that an amateur pianist could consistently produce anything even approaching the quality and sophistication of the great masters is nothing short of remarkable and may constitute the best evidence yet that the personality not only survives death, but may be capable of returning centuries after its demise to continue on with its life's work.

The Good-bye or Comfort Ghost

Perhaps the most common rationale for a personality manifesting to the still living remains the desire to say farewell. As such, the good-bye or comfort ghost is a manifestation that appears—often only once—to either say good-bye to a loved one or simply to send a signal that they are well and have passed over successfully.

An event from my own life provides a good example of this sort of ghostly phenomenon. In October of 1995 my stepfather was in the final stages of terminal cancer, during which time he expressed considerable trepidation about what would become of him after he died. Doing my best to reassure him that all would be well, he apparently took me at my word and experienced a reasonably comfortable, if protracted, passing. However, as if wanting to let my mother and siblings know he was okay, for weeks following his death he made us aware of his presence in a simple and nonintrusive way by turning the touch lamps in my mother's home on whenever she left the house.[11] At first it seemed a harmless prank, but eventually my mother grew increasingly exasperated at having to go through the house every evening turning each brightly burning fixture off. Finally tiring of my stepfather's apparent shenanigans, she eventually asked him to stop, after which the mysterious lighting ended, never to occur again. (Interestingly, she actually asked him to go "bother" one of her daughters, which—you guessed it—he did for a few more weeks by turning the lights on at her home before finally leaving permanently.)

It would be easy to assume a more prosaic explanation for this mystery than my stepfather's characteristically impish sense of humor manifesting itself from beyond the grave, but I find it curious that these lights (and there were several throughout the house) did not start coming on until after he died and ceased their bizarre behavior just as abruptly after my mother asked him to stop. Further, I could find no way to make the lights work without physically touching them (obviously, they work from the static charge in one's hand, corresponding nicely with some of the manifestation theories we discussed in the last chapter). I tried touching the lamps with other objects and pulled strings and other materials across them, but could only get them to light when I touched them with my hand. (I even watched a housefly land upon the base, but that too failed to get the fixture to light.) This led me to the inevitable conclusion that either my mother was unconsciously turning them on despite her insistence that she was not, that someone was breaking into her home only to turn the lights on (and leaving no other traces of their presence), or that somehow my late stepfather had found a way to electrically charge the fixtures as a means of saying good-bye. Whichever explanation one wishes to accept, the touch lamp phenomenon remains a good example of one way a personality might be able to manifest itself in a simple way in an attempt to remind others that they are still around.

---

11. For those unfamiliar with these appliances, touch lamps are small decorative light fixtures that are not turned on by tugging a chain or turning a knob as is common with most lights, but are instead turned on by lightly brushing the base of the lamp.

Of course, comfort ghosts can be more dramatic as well. Tales of widows seeing their late husband sitting on the foot of their bed or children encountering the manifestation of their dead sibling in their bedroom are legion, and even the ghost of a recently deceased family pet appearing has been occasionally reported. However, such reports must be examined within the context of the many ways grief can manifest itself in one's imagination to produce the very fantasy a bereaved loved one "needs" to bring closure to a tragic event. However, if all such occurrences are psychosomatically induced, they should be exceedingly common and, perhaps, even anticipated among grieving relatives, though that has not proven to be the case. Such instances are still relatively uncommon and, more often than not, entirely unexpected and sometimes even undesirable phenomenon, thereby reducing the chances that such visitations are hysteria-induced hallucinations. Trauma and excessive grief may account for some cases, but certainly not all of them.

The Curious Ghost

Ghosts that remain around for long periods of time and seem to be willing to appear to almost anyone could be caused by personalities who have found the ability to manifest so fascinating they purposely choose to haunt a location, their motive being not to say good-bye or settle some unfinished business, but simply to see what they can do.

Certainly the desire to experiment might be a powerful inducement to get a ghost to interact with the physical realm. I can imagine those personalities who in life demonstrated a considerable curiosity about the afterlife or were of a scientific mind might find the opportunity to manipulate matter and energy from the other side too good an opportunity to pass up. It is not inconceivable they may even be learning to manifest the necessary energy required to appear to us, honing their manifestation skills the same way an earthbound musician might hone their piano playing skills.

Perhaps there are even paranormal investigators working the equation from the other side, so to speak, and are hard at work attempting to prove the existence of the spiritual realm as doggedly as some ghost hunters are trying to do from this side. Reports of deceased paranormal investigators trying to communicate with their previous colleagues and students are not unknown, making it perhaps only a matter of time before the spiritual and physical realms come together to produce irrefutable proof that human consciousness survives the death of the brain that houses it, thereby forcing science to start from scratch in defining what constitutes reality.

I would suspect such personalities, however, to be fairly rare and frequently frustrated in their efforts to get through to us "thick mortals," perhaps making them prone to tiring of the game and moving on to explore other realms of the spirit. After all, if they are curious enough to attempt to manifest within linear time and space, we can assume they might just as easily grow curious enough about other aspects of the ethereal realm to abandon their haunting experiments and move on. Thus, while curious ghosts might prove the most likely type to help us demonstrate the existence of a spiritual realm, they may also be among the most "flighty" in that the very curiosity that makes them willing to try to communicate with us makes them equally likely to leave to explore other aspects of their new existence as well.

The Mischievous Ghost

Similar to the curious ghost but of a somewhat more menacing vein is the mischievous or "playful" ghost. It is different from the curious ghost in that it is not as interested in demonstrating the reality of the supernatural realm as much as it simply enjoys frightening the still living.

Obviously, such ghosts are immature and childish (like the personalities behind them) and are comparable to the practical joker who thinks everything he does is hilarious and cannot understand why others refuse to see the humor in his often mean-spirited and usually embarrassing shenanigans. It can also be among the most frightening type of ghost in that it is actually *trying* to scare people (whereas most ghosts do so unintentionally). This can manifest itself in something as innocent as making a chair rock, hiding a piece of jewelry, or pulling the sheets off a bed, or to something as serious as tugging on a person's hair, slapping, or even tripping! Clearly, they are, at a minimum, the most difficult sort to live with, for they *want* to make a nuisance of themselves and, in fact, go out of their way to make living with them almost impossible.

Additionally, being that these are very interactive ghosts, they may be the source of at least some (if not all) poltergeist activity. This is not a popular theory, however, for poltergeists are usually thought of as uncontrolled bursts of telekinetic energy put out by a particular living person. However, as with most ghostly theories, it could just as well be that mischievous ghosts are able to utilize the traumatic energy such a person puts out to move things; in other words, a nervous teenage girl may simply be the perfect conduit for a playful spirit by inadvertently providing the very energy it requires to do its mischief, without which it would be unable to manifest itself. This would explain why poltergeist activity frequently ceases when the "source energy" leaves the vicinity of the activity (the entity no longer has the prerequisite source of energy). It also explains why poltergeist activity sometimes follows the individual to other places (the ghost is attracted to their energy and follows them). Of course, this does not explain why all similarly high-strung teenagers don't attract such negative energies. One possibility is that such ghosts are themselves exceedingly rare or that people put out different psychic energies and mischievous entities are attracted to only certain types (or, perhaps, frequencies?). In any case, the idea that there are personalities willing to pull stunts on the still living should be no more remarkable than the fact that such fortunately uncommon individuals exist in the physical realm today. An immature personality is no more likely to suddenly "grow up" once he or she is dead than a mature one is to revert to its second childhood once it dies. People will always be people, after all, regardless of whether they are dead or alive.

The Angry Ghost

While a mischievous ghost might be, at its heart, relatively benign and even potentially amusing at times, an angry ghost is another matter. Negative energy is a powerful force in its own right, so the idea that anger, rage, and hatred might keep a personality earthbound has to be considered. Certainly people have been willing to endure tremendous hardship and great personal loss in the quest for revenge, so the thought that an angry personality might be willing to endure the personal hell of an earthly wandering in search of vengeance is not difficult to imagine, and in fact, would be entirely consistent with what we know of human nature.

How the manifestation of an angry entity would look and feel is a source for considerable debate; it could be as simple as an oppressive or uncomfortable feeling one gets upon entering a particular room to something as frightening as an air of overpowering hatred and dread hanging in the atmosphere.[12] In more extreme cases, it may even manifest poltergeist-like activity and do things like hurl objects or even physically attack a person, so the ability of an angry ghost to do real damage should not be minimized.

What's important to recognize about an angry ghost, however, is the fact that it has gotten itself so deeply enmeshed within the periphery of the physical realm that it is truly stuck and, in some cases, may be entirely incapable of moving on to higher planes of existence (without, perhaps, considerable help from other spiritual entities).

We will look more at this issue later, but for now it is enough to understand that of all the reasons a person might have for becoming a ghost, the desire for revenge and the need to wreak havoc among the still living is the most disastrous and the one we should most strive to avoid. It is a self-defeating and even self-destructive rationale that never truly sates the angry ghost's thirst for revenge, but only compounds his or her problems in the spiritual realm. Fortunately such entities are relatively rare, it seems, but even so they present the great-

---

12. I recount an encounter with an angry or "evil" entity in more detail in chapter 8.

est challenge to the ghost hunter, for they truly are capable of being dangerous, especially if one feeds into their anger by sending out the very negative emotions one is sensing from them. Anger is a destructive force that grows more powerful with time and can only be dissipated through the power of love and compassion. Could this be the reason most religions teach the importance of forgiveness and controlling one's anger? Could our ancient religious beliefs understand on some subliminal level the overwhelmingly negative consequences that moving into the spiritual realm encased within hatred could entail, and could the need for repentance and forgiveness taught by many religions, then, be a means of saving us not from hell or God's wrath but from ourselves and decades or even centuries of pointless spiritual wandering?

Conclusion

It should be obvious by now that there are many reasons for becoming a ghost, most of them having to do with human nature and our base personality flaws. Everything from love and concern for those left behind to curiosity and immaturity to outright hatred for the living are all reasons anyone could become—at least briefly—a ghost. In that regard, then, becoming a ghost appears to be something that can be both voluntary or accidental and, in some cases, may even be unconscious. This is why it is important that we be conscious of our own foibles, attachments, and resentments, for they could be the mechanism by which we too may one day experience existence within the context of a wandering spiritual entity. As such, introspection should be an important part of our earthly existence, for in the long run the "soul work" we accomplish here while in the flesh may have far greater repercussions in eternity than we can imagine.

On the other hand, it also seems likely that most people will never become a ghost but will instead choose to move on immediately after they die, precisely as they were designed to do. But for those who do not, remaining behind carries its own special kind of purgatory, for they will be extremely limited and often incapable of interacting with the very world they so badly long to still be a part of. For them, time becomes a trap and the physical realm a prison of their own making. To find oneself in such a state may be the ultimate wrong turn and one that may take years, decades, or even centuries to be rescued from.

Of course, this doesn't mean the universe forgets about them. I am convinced there are spiritual energies out there whose job it is to wean the more confused and reluctant spirits away from the physical realm and gently guide them home. For some, however, such assistance will not be wanted or appreciated, and the battle may rage for some time before such entities are willing to be led to safety. But, then, it is the function of the eternal to restore and heal lost souls, just as it is the nature of God to love and respect each personality and the person it represents enough to show each of them the way home. This remains the best demonstration of the power of love, for there is no more powerful force in the universe and, in fact, may be all that truly exists within the realm of the absolute.

chapter six

Some Post-Haunting Scenarios

A necdotal evidence suggests that if ghosts exist at all, they certainly do not seem to hang around long. Most hauntings and ghostly encounters have what is known as a "life span"; that is, a period of time during which manifestations occur before they permanently cease. In fact, most manifestations do not repeat their single appearance or, if they do, inevitably they cease doing so within a few months. Others, however, are like orbiting comets and can exhibit active periods lasting for years, decades, and, in a few rare cases, even centuries.[13] For the most part, however, the norm seems to be that most ghosts are here today and gone tomorrow—sometimes quite literally.

This, of course, brings up the question of what finally becomes of ghosts. Do they eventually fade into nothingness or do they move on to some final spiritual estate, and, if they do move on, do they continue to exist in some recognizable form or do they transform into something else completely different?

It's an important issue to address, for we are not just dealing with mere theories here, but with the eternal fate of real people we have known and loved. Additionally, it is an important question to examine for ourselves as well, for each of us will one day confront this issue

---

13. There are residences believed to have been haunted for centuries, but it is often difficult to determine whether it is the same ghost doing the haunting, or if the residence itself just seems to be a natural magnet for paranormal energy that is capable of manifesting multiple entities over the years.

personally, making it a determining factor in deciding whether we look upon our own impending physical death with fear and dread, or with curiosity, wonderment, and even anticipation. As such, in this chapter we will explore a number of theories about the possible fate of ghosts, from both a practical and spiritual standpoint, which have been put forward by ghost hunters, mediums, parapsychologists, religionists, and others over the years. Obviously, we can't know with any degree of certainty what finally happens to the spirits of those who have gone before us from our limited perspective on this side of eternity, and so inevitably this material must remain highly speculative, yet even then it may still contain much within it to consider. Further, there is no right or wrong answer, for much of what rings true is going to be determined by environmental conditioning and personal preferences and biases; the religious person, for example, is going to have a much different idea about our postmortem existence than a secularist might maintain, for both are approaching the subject from very different perspectives. In the end, it should become apparent that there is no final verdict to render, for it is up to each individual to choose for themselves which scenario or "final estate" strikes them as the most plausible.

The Annihilation Hypothesis

Proponents of the annihilation theory are quite willing to allow for the possibility that human consciousness may survive the demise of the brain, but consider this ability to be only a short-term phenomena. In this theory, human consciousness is not unlike embers from a blazing fire that may continue to glow for some time after the fire has gone out before eventually growing dark and cold. In effect, the personality is like a flashlight that grows dimmer as its batteries grow weaker, with its life span being determined by such factors as the strength and determination of the energy involved as well as possible environmental factors such as humidity, heat, and the availability of usable energy. Of course, just as some flashlight batteries last considerably longer than others, so too might consciousness fade at different rates, but eventually it is doomed to ultimately join the body in death and wink out of existence.

The problem with this idea, however, is that it is little more than an attempt to cobble together materialistic science's insistence on the temporal nature of consciousness with the paranormalist's belief that personality survives physical death, with neither side ending up satisfied with the results. Either the personality survives the physical demise of the brain or it does not. If the consciousness survives physical death at all, it is then operating independently of the brain through some as-yet-unknown mechanism, making the assumption that it will eventually cease to do so unfounded and untenable. If the mind can exist apart from the brain in any capacity, there is no logical reason to imagine it is not capable of doing so indefinitely. It simply doesn't follow that it should.

Further, if souls exist for only a short time before fading into nothingness, this effectively eliminates the spiritual realm in its entirety. Instead of us living in a never-ending universe of pure energy, it would be replaced by a universe of absolute entropy in which energy is being drained down into a state of utter uselessness until, in the end, nothing finally exists in any useful form. It is the ultimate nihilistic approach to spirituality that promises only a cold, dark eternity for everything, making even this brief span of time we spend on this planet, in many ways, a huge waste of time. If someone wishes to maintain this theory with any tenacity, I leave it to them. I, for one, find it to be little more than another attempt to steer the car back onto the materialist's track for no particularly good reason other than the desire to forge a compromise between those who accept the possibility of postmortem survival and those who do not.

The Heaven or Hell Hypothesis

A somewhat more universally accepted theory is that ghosts (and all souls in general, be they ghosts or not) eventually move on to another plane of existence, though what this state might be remains, of course, highly subjective and purely conjectural. Within most religions—especially those prevalent in the West—the "final estate" is summed up in two words: heaven—the abode of the righteous, repentant, good, and/or deserving—and hell—the place reserved for the wicked or unrepentant.

Which destination the soul finds itself in is, at least according to tradition, a result of the decisions each person has made during their lifetime, with some being rewarded for their goodness and others being punished for their evil. There are variations on this theme, of course; some religions don't believe that good and bad acts are weighed against each other, but that one's belief in the right things versus the wrong things (such as embracing the correct religion or accepting Jesus as one's savior) are examined. Others also teach the existence of an intermediary state between heaven and hell in which the fallen but redeemable soul may work off its sin debt in a type of limbo world (frequently referred to as purgatory) and so make itself worthy of eventually entering heaven. Still others don't believe in a literal hell at all, but consider it a metaphor for the simple extermination of the soul.

Obviously there are as many ideas about these concepts as there are colors in the rainbow, but for now it is enough to briefly consider the strengths and weaknesses of each idea. Since the belief that the soul goes to heaven remains the most popular and enduring of all theories, we will start there.

The Case for Heaven

It is probably safe to say that most New Agers and those who believe in the postmortem existence perceive the spiritual realm to be a place of light and beauty, so it can be said that heaven exists naturally as a matter of course. In effect, to be out of the body is to be in heaven, just as to be underwater makes one automatically wet. However, the kind of heaven most people imagine when they hear the word is the type that has been generally portrayed by religion, which is a "place" one goes (as opposed to a condition one experiences naturally as a byproduct of being outside the body). As such, we will deal here exclusively with the more traditional concept of heaven as taught by modern theologians.

First, it is important to understand this type of heaven is generally considered a possibility only for "good" people and, as such, a place only some ghosts go. This effectively makes heaven a symbol of justice rather than merely a spiritual abode, for it makes one's eventual ascension there dependent upon events and decisions made while in the flesh. We will look at this construct in more detail in a moment, but for now let us confine the debate to merely considering a "place" called heaven and see how it stands up to logic.

If we accept the premise that the "good" or worthy soul eventually wings its way to heaven, the first question that must be asked is just what is the soul's purpose in going there? In effect, what is heaven for? Does one go there specifically to enjoy a sort of Edenic existence throughout eternity in a place of never-ending ease and relaxation, with the soul eternally encased within a world of perfect harmony and love, or is it to be considered a place of learning, growth, and introspection? In other words, is there something to do there other than merely enjoy one's pleasant surroundings, or is that enough in and of itself?

While this concept appeals to most people, I would personally find such an idyllic existence, no matter how peaceful and pleasant it might be, problematic. I should think that after a time (although time, at least as we understand the concept, would not exist there) it would become almost unbearably dull until eventually it became more akin to a plush, luxurious prison than anything else. While I can understand the attractiveness of such a place to people who have had to work hard all their life, for those who believe the universe to be a place of growth and self-discovery, it has little to offer beyond a routine mired in mind-numbing sameness and a brain stuck in neutral throughout eternity. Much as a two-week cruise can start out relaxing and enjoyable, by the end of the second week one usually starts to become anxious to disembark and return to the "real" world of family, career, and life in general.

Of course, many people see heaven in broader terms and imagine that we continue to learn and grow there spiritually and intellectually just as we did on Earth. In effect, we continue on in heaven much as we did on Earth, only now without the limitations, hindrances, temptations, and obstacles we were forced to contend with here in the flesh. This concept, then, makes heaven, in essence, little more than an idealized Earth with none of the problems and all the time in the world to learn what we should have been learning while on Earth.

While I am perfectly content with the idea that there would undoubtedly be much to learn and see in such a place, I'm not sure how one would be able to grow spiritually there. Growth comes about through overcoming the obstacles life throws our way and rising to new challenges it places before us. But how are such experiences even possible in an Edenic environment like heaven? If heaven is a place of love and light, as most people imagine, it is difficult to see what mechanism might be in place that would allow us to grow in any appreciable way. It just doesn't seem set up for it.

In an effort to circumvent this possibility, some have suggested that heaven might be a type of "simulator" where one can construct virtual realities in their mind—entire worlds in which a person might manufacture the various challenges that would help them grow—and so continue to mature in that way. Such, however, seems to be a dishonest means of doing so. In such a scenario we would have to know that any situation or crisis we might construct would be merely illusory and so incapable of ever providing any real sense of accomplishment (or failure, for that matter.) Just as war games, regardless of how realistic they may appear, can never truly capture the terror and horror of actual combat, so too does it seem unlikely that an "Earth/life simulator" could ever bring about the kind of growth only a bout in the physical realm can produce. We *need* the physical realm to grow, potentially making heaven even something of an impediment to achieving that goal. It is only when we are put into situations that call for genuine patience, perseverance, and resourcefulness that real growth is possible.

The only way a permanent heaven would work, then, is if spiritual maturation is not the goal at all, but simply a positive byproduct of a life lived well. However, does this not make any efforts at bettering oneself essentially a waste of time, since heaven is not particularly interested in one's level of spiritual maturity? It's akin to imagining everyone automatically receiving a million dollars on their fortieth birthday regardless of how much or little they worked throughout their life. Under such circumstances, working hard would simply have no point and, in fact, could even be considered a foolish waste of time, thus potentially encouraging spiritual apathy.

The Case for Hell

The opposite of heaven is, of course, hell (a place that has always proven and continues to remain especially popular among religious conservatives of all faiths). Not remarkably, however, it too comes complete with its own set of problems.

The biggest problem with the concept of a place of eternal punishment and torment is that if we accept the premise that the spiritual realm is essentially a place of love and light, it is difficult to see how one might find themselves in a locale where precisely the opposite conditions exist. Additionally, if we are serious about the notion that God is love, the idea that there exists a place of eternal torment within "his" realm is inconsistent with that notion, at least if we correctly perceive just what love is.

This is a point that cannot be overlooked. How we interpret the word "love" has tremendous bearing on whether we are able to accept the idea that there exists a hell. If we interpret love as an emotion—a feeling of affection, sentimentality, or even compassion—the idea that God might lose those feelings toward some of the more rebellious examples of his creation is not out of the question, making the idea that there could be a place of punishment set aside for such individuals not out of the question. However, if we define love not as an emotion but as an ongoing, unchanging, and unchangeable attitude and see love as a universal force or constant that is continually working to bring all things together, to heal all wounds, and to restore everything to a state of radiant perfection, then hell is out of the question, for it would stand directly in opposition to this purpose. As such, hell as a state of eternal punishment for the wicked or unrepentant cannot exist as long as we maintain the illusion that God is love.

But what of justice, some will ask. After all, people have done some pretty terrible things and need to be held accountable, so wouldn't God be merely giving lip service to the idea of justice and morality if he refused to hold accountable those who reject his love and do harm to others? In other words, can God be truly loving without being fair and just at the same time? And, for that matter, what of those who utterly reject God and do not want to be integrated into the greater whole? Doesn't God have to take their decision to reject him seriously?

First, only human beings are capable of maintaining the contradiction that one can be both loving and just at the same time; in reality, the two concepts are incompatible. If one is merciful and loving to those who have done evil, there can be no justice if they are forgiven. By the same token, if justice prevails and one is punished according to their sins, there is no room for love to operate, for justice has supplanted it. Therefore, which position one holds will determine whether God is, indeed, a being of unconditional love or one who merely professes to be. There is no other option open to us.

Second, we have to recognize that what constitutes "sin" or the rejection of God is often an arbitrary opinion based on established cultural norms and changing public perceptions. Public attitudes shift with each generation and vary among cultures, making it increasingly difficult to define "sin" at all. Whereas once premarital sex, homosexuality, prostitution, and divorce were considered unforgivable sins against God, now most Westerners would consider such acts less heinous and, in the case of genetically induced homosexuality, outside the realm of being considered a sin at all. Even such presumed absolutes as murder are frequently overlooked in the context of self-defense and war, while definitions of what even constitutes murder have become blurred when one gets into the areas of abortion, euthanasia, and suicide. As such, what we believe people ought to be punished for changes with the times, rendering any arguments about justice problematic at best.

But what of those who do commit crimes we can universally consider wrong, such as stealing, lying, and cold-blooded murder? Again, we have to take into account one's environment and the unique circumstances that may have shaped his or her development. Can we really hold a man born into a ruthless world accountable for his brutality if that is all he has known from the womb? Can a woman really be held accountable for being a prostitute if that is the only means she believes she has of supporting herself? Obviously, there are many variables that need to be taken into account when defining sin and the need for punishment, and we would be wise to tread carefully, lest the "mote in our own eye"[14] be made readily apparent.

Finally, even if God does not hold us accountable for our sins, that does not mean we may not experience the consequences of our actions, both in this life and in the one to come. We all have heard stories of people who live a hellish life of addiction and criminality largely as a result of their own poor choices and neglect, so it is difficult to maintain that anyone gets off "scot-free" under any circumstances. Negative consequences seem to be woven into the very fabric of life itself, making it rare for any individual to truly avoid the pain inherent to their evil or selfish deeds (even if those consequences are realized through nothing worse than a lifetime of guilt and regret).

And as far as the spiritual realm goes, some teach that the mind itself may be its own worst tormentor and that it is quite possible that a person may experience a type of hell within the context of their own tormented imagination. In other words, a person may create a hell for themselves within their own mind and continue to experience that as

---

14. Matthew 7:3–5. Parallels Luke 6:41–42. "Mote" is roughly translated as a splinter or piece of dried grass.

their reality within the spiritual realm for a considerable period of time. While this may be, for all practical matters, similar to what it is assumed one might experience in the context of a traditional understanding of hell, the difference is that this hell does not exist in the world of absolute reality, but only within the imagination. Further, it is neither eternal nor externally imposed, making one free to discard it at any time and walk out of its "fires" into the realm of pure light whenever they wish. That some may choose not to do so is not an indictment of God, but of themselves.

As such, the entire concept of hell, besides being inconsistent with the idea of a God of love or a spiritual realm of wholeness and peace, is untenable from a moral and logical perspective and appears to be more a product of our own fears and prejudices than of anything that might exist in the realm of pure spirit. This would make it something we need not worry about in regard to those loved ones who may have died at their own hand or who passed over with something of a less than sterling character to contend with. The spiritual realm is about learning from our errors, not punishing us for our very human failings. It is about growth, and that can never be accomplished from within the context of a jail cell or a torture chamber.

Other Spiritual Realms and Dimensions

Those who do not maintain a belief in a literal heaven or hell generally favor the theory that the soul ultimately transcends our limited realm of being and ascends to other planes or dimensions of existence, from where it is no longer capable of interacting within the physical realm. In other words, once loved ones have ascended to a higher plane, they lose the ability to manifest within our physical plane and so appear, at least from our perspective, as if they no longer exist. A ghost, then, is simply a soul that has not entirely made that transition yet and is either reluctant to move on for some reason or is hesitating while it finishes some unresolved issues in this dimension. Then, once it has accomplished its mission or has become adequately acclimated to its new existence or convinced of the need to move on, it departs our plane of existence to emerge into a new one, at which point it seems to fade into nothingness.

What occurs on these other planes of existence is, of course, impossible to ascertain. One theory is that we simply emerge into another dimension very similar to our own, but one that appears from our perspective as solid and material as ours does to us now. This, in effect, could lead to the possibility that there is an "alternate" universe that exists entirely outside our ability to perceive it, but one that is every bit as real as our own. In fact, this idea even suggests the possibility that there could be literally thousands of dimensions (or alternate universes) coexisting alongside each other and that each is populated by souls that perceive their reality to be the only true one. Like primitive tribesmen who imagine their tiny jungle enclave to be the only world that exists, so too might we be experiencing only one very tiny piece of a much more vast reality in which literally trillions upon trillions of beings populate many billions of alternate universes at the same time, each existing within different contexts and at varying vibrational levels simultaneously, yet each entirely unaware of other planes of existence beyond their own.

Of course, this may be a bit complex for some people and perhaps even entirely unnecessary; I offer it only as an example of how "ultimate reality" may be far more grand than we can begin to imagine— much less comprehend. For all I know, this single universe may be it, but then it was not too long ago that most people presumed our planet to be the only one in the universe capable of sustaining life. Perceptions change in the world of science and philosophy all the time, so why not in the realm of eternity as well?

The Reincarnation Hypothesis

The fifth theory concerning the eventual disposition of the soul, and one that has been growing in popularity over the past few years, is the idea that souls return to the earthly realm after a brief period of rest and reflection so they can continue to pursue their mission of spiritual maturation and growth—known popularly as reincarnation. In this scenario, the consciousness merely hovers about the spiritual realm for a time, perhaps spending time reviewing its previous incarnation and deciding upon its next earthly venue, before finally immersing itself into the density of matter once again. A ghost, then, is merely a consciousness that is "dragging its feet" for a time until it finally tires of its noncorporeal existence and is ready to move on to its next incarnation.

While a controversial idea, it has much going for it, at least from the perspective of eternity. First, it supports the idea that the soul is a transitory entity embarked on a journey of spiritual growth designed to ultimately reintegrate it with the divine source of the universe, while also acknowledging the soul's inherent immortality and incorruptibility. Secondly, it is a perfect mechanism for achieving spiritual growth, for by introducing the soul to many incarnations—each of them lived within the context of different genders, economic circumstances, and physical venues—it is certain to grow in wisdom and knowledge as it experiences new challenges and opportunities within each lifetime. And, finally, it works well within the context of love, for as the soul matures it moves closer to reintegration with the divine, thus bringing purpose and function to the entire creation.

While there are many who reject reincarnation for various scientific, religious, or cultural reasons, it does explain nicely why ghosts eventually disappear from our physical realm and what becomes of them. While it does not explain what becomes of the individual personalities each soul manifests while on this planet, it does bring a degree of cohesion and internal consistency to the process, and it is further supported by some empirical evidence in the form of conscious, past-life recollections in children and verifiable events gleaned from hypnotically induced regression memories in adults. Though this book is not the proper venue within which to discuss the evidence for reincarnation with anything approaching thoroughness, the fact is that the case for reincarnation is growing all the time. I would strongly urge any reader genuinely interested in the subject of postmortem existence to study this concept more thoroughly from both a scientific and spiritual perspective, for it has much to say to both the human condition and to the entire issue of life after death.[15]

Conclusion

While there is probably no way of ascertaining with any degree of certainty what ultimately happens to our loved ones when they finally pass on, we can rest in the assurance that whatever it is, the universe is a safe and loving place that has only their best interests at heart. Ghosts are simply those who have yet to recognize or trust that idea or who are not quite ready to let go of a physical life they can no longer experience or appreciate because of anger, sadness, fear, or an unwillingness to accept the inevitable. The process goes on regardless of their beliefs (or lack of them), for we are dealing with a very big universe and a very big God.

We are all parts of a greater whole, and one day we will each come to recognize that fact and take our place within the divine realm of pure being, for there is nowhere else we ultimately may go and nothing else we may ultimately do. Whether we recognize this fact while still in the flesh or after we have passed may have much to say in determining whether we might become ghosts ourselves or move on to our next plane of existence with confidence in the process and faith in the divine.

---

15. For a fairly thorough and straightforward treatment of the evidence for and the mechanics of reincarnation, I would refer you to my book *Mystery of Reincarnation* (Llewellyn Publishing, 2005). For a good scientific study of the issue, I recommend any of the works of Dr. Ian Stevenson as well as others included in the bibliography.

part two

Ghost Hunting 101

It may surprise the reader to learn that ghost hunting is a genuine science that maintains its own arsenal of equipment and strategies all designed to scientifically prove the existence of ghosts, and as we would be ill-equipped to discuss the subject intelligently without a clear understanding of just what these tools are and what they are supposed to do, it is important we go off on a little tangent and take a look at how paranormal investigators go about looking for these beings.

While at first glance this might seem an unwarranted diversion from the main topic, it is important to understand the science of ghost hunting if we are ever to begin understanding precisely what a ghost might be. It is not enough to merely define one's quarry and move on. The "tools of the trade," so to speak, can tell us many things about these beings, everything from their physical makeup to the mechanics of manifestation, so it is well worth our time to understand what these tools are, how they are used, and what they are trying to do if we are to acquire a clearer understanding of this phenomenon.

We will also have the opportunity to learn about their limitations and potential pitfalls as well, which will help us gain an appreciation as to why it is so hard to prove the existence of ghosts despite the sophistication of the technology at our disposal and the technical acumen of those who use it. Perhaps in the end, it may very well be that only in understanding why ghosts are so difficult to capture with modern equipment that we will begin to gain a clearer understanding of the precise nature of the phenomenon we are dealing with.

chapter seven

The Tools of the Trade

In the summer of 1984 a clever little comedy called *Ghostbusters*—an unlikely but fun romp about three somewhat unscrupulous paranormal researchers who team up to exterminate unwanted ghosts—hit the theaters to become one of the surprise hits of the year. While the movie, teaming the comedic genius of Bill Murray, Dan Akroyd, and Harold Ramis, entertained audiences with its bizarre and engaging characters and amusing story line, it also managed to bring a bit of techno-fun to the screen in the form of a host of exotic and unlikely devices our heroes made use of in their ongoing efforts at trapping and containing the mischievous and often disgusting spiritual entities that infested New York City. Using everything from unlicensed nuclear accelerators to magnetic "ghost traps" designed to actually contain a spiritual entity within a metal box, crowds howled at the antics of the trio as they scoured the city in their round-the-clock quest to rid the physical world of the unwanted refuse of the ethereal realm. They even had a massive magnetic containment chamber where they stored the trapped spiritual entities until, of course, it was shut down by an EPA bureaucrat, thus opening the gates to all sorts of paranormal mischief as the entities escaped en masse.

Of course, real ghost hunters do not have access to such exotic (and potentially dangerous) equipment to aid them in their research, nor, of course, are most of them in the business of ridding a residence of a spirit, though there are those that do offer that service. Instead, they must get by with far more prosaic tools in their ongoing effort to locate their invisible quarry. In many cases, however, these can be just as interesting as anything the *Ghostbusters* made use of. As such, in this chapter we will take a brief look at the equipment real paranormal researchers use in an effort to both understand exactly what these tools do as well as what limits them from being as useful to the researcher as they could be. This will allow us to see how the science of "ghost hunting" is carried out, for it turns out that the hunt for evidence of paranormal activity itself can be the most fascinating and exciting part of the entire adventure.

The first thing one should realize is that ghost hunting is not cheap—at least, not if one wants to do it right. It takes more than a good camera and a strong disposition; it usually requires a virtual arsenal of often costly devices (along with many hours of practice to make the equipment useful) to do the job. Unfortunately, the average layman may be entirely unaware of how sophisticated this equipment must be, for the serious paranormal investigators are engaged in genuine science, regardless of what their critics contend, and are as intent upon obtaining empirical, scientifically valid evidence as would be any scientist testing a new theory. As such, it is vital to understand the kinds of equipment the researcher is using, how it works, and what it is supposed to do if we are to base our belief—or disbelief—in ghosts on anything beyond pure opinion.

To begin, it is initially necessary to recognize that paranormal researchers approach their quarry from the presumption that ghosts are basically units of energy capable of manifesting themselves in our physical realm through the use of some mechanism we are as yet unfamiliar with. This ability to interact within the physical universe, then, should be detectable to the proper equipment, and, as such, most of an investigator's equipment is made up of devices designed to detect electrical or thermal changes in the environment. They also make considerable use of audio equipment in an effort to detect any speech or other noises a ghost may manifest, as well as operate a whole range of video equipment and cameras in an attempt to capture a ghostly image on film or videotape. While we will look at the lesser known environmental detectors later, we will begin our study with the most well-known, as well as most controversial, piece of gear the ghost hunter has at his or her disposal: the camera.

Photographing a Ghost: The Trials and Tribulations of Spirit Photography

Photographs of alleged ghosts (better known as spirit photography) goes back to the advent of the photographic process, when developers first began noticing ghostly images appearing unexpectedly on photographic plates during development. These were usually explainable by the nature of early photo taking itself, when images were burned onto a negative in a timed process lasting anywhere from several seconds to many minutes (or, in some cases, even hours). This not only demanded that the subject remain rigidly still while the shutter was open, but also made those who moved during the process blurry and somewhat translucent (or even "ghostly") in appearance. Other anomalies were the result of double exposures, when a photographic plate was inadvertently used twice, leaving a very clear double image on the plate or negative. Despite such prosaic explanations for such anomalies, however, there were those who insisted that such images were actually spirits of the long departed. Since photography was a new technology to most people and spiritism[16] was becoming hugely popular at the time, it wasn't difficult to convince many that these semisolid images were ghosts caught on film, and a cottage industry, spirit photography, was born.

Unfortunately, some unscrupulous photographers looking to pad their meager incomes and realizing that people were willing to pay exorbitant fees for the chance of having their portrait taken with a ghost, began not only purposely manipulating the process for enhanced

---

16. Spiritism is the practice of contacting the dead, usually through the services of a medium via a séance, which proved especially popular in America and Europe throughout the later half of the nineteenth and early years of the twentieth centuries.

effect, but began staging spirit visitations (where an appropriately garbed assistant hovered about in the background while a portrait was being taken), all in an effort to take advantage of the general public's unfamiliarity with the technology behind photography and their willingness to believe. This made spirit photography a lucrative profession, resulting in the production of literally hundreds of often laughably bad, faked spirit photos. Consequently, despite being a fairly harmless (though not necessarily cheap) con, it did manage to do incalculable harm to real paranormal research. In fact, no single scam did more to discredit "ghost hunting" in the eyes of science, with the possible exception of charlatan mediums producing third-rate seances, than did these entrepreneurs.

We may shake our heads today at the naïveté of those who fell for such nonsense a hundred years ago, but we are not all that far removed from our ghost-believing ancestors as we would like to think. Faked photos of ghosts are still being made today despite the vast improvements in photography and our better understanding of the process, forcing science to be, as it should, extremely leery of even the best spirit photos. It is entirely too easy to fake a convincing ghost photo, especially considering the vastly improved skills of the hoaxer as compared to his or her nineteenth-century counterparts, as well as the array of photo manipulation technologies on the market today. Therefore, it is probable that no still photo will ever be readily accepted as evidence of the existence of a ghost, though that does not prevent the determined ghost hunter from trying their best to capture an entity on film.

However, just as spirit photos are easier to fake than ever before, such fakes are also easier to detect than they were even a few decades ago. Careful researchers know what to look for in faked photos (many have even tried producing their own and so are familiar with how easily it can be done)[17] thus making it increasingly difficult for a hoaxer to fool the competent investigator. Further, photography has come a long way since the early days of black-and-white prints being made

---

17. See example on page 101 for a step-by-step demonstration of how a ghost photo can be faked with a little imagination and the right software.

How to produce a ghost photo

(in five easy steps)

Step 1: Photo of author's son next to his car.

Step 2: Photo of author in an appropriately ghostly pose.

Step 3: Cutout of author brought into original photo.

Step 4: Cutout photo is smudged and blurred for a more ghostly effect.

Step 5: Cutout is made transparent and placed in proper position. Level of opacity can be adjusted as necessary to achieve desired effect.

from glass plates. Today the average investigator is likely to make use of not only a high-end 35mm color camera with all the bells and whistles, but a high-quality digital camera and, in many cases, infrared and 3-D cameras as well (as well as an array of video and high-speed film cameras). Therefore, he or she is not only better equipped to capture an entity on film or videotape than at any time in history, but is more competent and capable of determining the plausibility of any photo that comes their way. Of course, this doesn't mean that even professional investigators are incapable of being fooled by a very good fake or, more commonly, of fooling themselves into seeing a ghostly manifestation in a swirl of smoke where none exists. After all, paranormal researchers are only human and can often be as biased as everyone else. And, since most are already favorably disposed toward the idea of ghosts, it sometimes doesn't take much to delude themselves into believing they have a genuine "capture."[18] Yet even then, their results must pass muster with an army of other researchers and hard-nosed skeptics before it can be considered legitimate, thus giving a photo that can successfully traverse such a gauntlet a better pedigree than most.

Types of Visible Ghostly Manifestations

Before we examine the array of different video devices paranormal investigators use, it is first necessary that we understand the process of photographing ghosts. It is something of a misnomer to assume an investigator simply traipses about a darkened house in the middle of the night until he spots some sort of ghostly manifestation and then aims his camera and shoots away. Ghosts are almost never that obvious. Further, investigators rarely if ever actually see a ghost appear before them; most manifestations are often only noticed later when they appear on the developed film. More often than not, investigators wait—usually for hours at a time—for some anomaly in the environment (such as a sudden "cold spot" or heightened electromagnetic readings to appear on their instruments) and then begin taking a series

---

18. A "capture" is the current term for a ghost photo thought to be legitimate.

of photos in the general area of the aberration. Usually they have no idea if they will capture anything on film (usually they do not), which is what makes photographing a ghost such a difficult process. Like playing the slots in Vegas, it can take many hours to hit the jackpot, but once it does hit, the payoff can be extraordinary.

Second, it is important to understand exactly what it is the researcher is looking to capture on film. Obviously the investigator is trying to obtain a picture of a ghost, but what constitutes photographic evidence of a ghost is not always clear. As such, it is necessary that we look at the various types of ghostly manifestations investigators have catalogued over the years and the many theories used to account for them.

Ghostly images are generally divided into three categories: orbs, vortexes, and full body manifestations. We will look at each in turn (and in ascending order of rarity) and consider the most common explanations for each usually forwarded by the skeptical community to explain them away.

Orbs

An orb is basically a ball of light that appears unexpectedly in a photo. Normally white or bluish in color, one or more may appear on an otherwise normal photograph and are occasionally captured on videotape as well (in which case they are usually moving, often at a high rate of speed). Not remarkably, the paranormal camp is divided on whether these little specks of light are genuinely paranormal in nature, are naturally occurring electrical phenomena (akin to ball lightning), or are nothing at all.

The first camp (those that consider orbs to be paranormal manifestations) hypothesizes that orbs are very basic manifestations of spiritual energy in its simplest and most primitive form, with an orb being nothing less than a ghost in its earliest or most primordial stage of manifesting. In essence, one could think of orbs as "tiny ghosts" moving around a room, their essence being contained within a tiny sphere of pure energy, like air inside a bubble.

This appears to be a popular notion within the paranormal community and the one most popular with amateur (and some seasoned) ghost hunters as well, but, as I said, it is not the only theory. Some paranormal researchers consider orbs to be naturally occurring electrical phenomenon, though the science behind this contention is not entirely clear. If it is a form of ball lightning or some other type of electrical discharge, it appears capable of forming quite spontaneously, unlike their better known cousins, making this theory more problematic than explanatory and, as such, less popular or as widespread as others.

In the end, many researchers reject both theories and simply dismiss orbs as lens flare or reflections of light off airborne particles such as dust, snow, drizzle, or even insects that have wandered in front of the camera just as the flash goes off. They correctly point out that many times pictures of orbs are taken in dusty, dark rooms where the smallest particles of airborne material can reflect the flash of a camera and so stand out in stark contrast to the darkness of the background. In the hands of inexperienced or overly enthusiastic ghost hunters, then, every blob of light on a photo thus becomes a "ghost," much to the chagrin of their more careful and somber colleagues.

That most orbs are flash reflections off some airborne particle of dust is probably valid, and most orb photos undoubtedly can be explained away as such. However, there are those who insist on accepting at least some orbs as ghostly manifestations, pointing out that they are sometimes found on photos that did not use a flash or are taken during the day. It is also difficult to understand why, if orbs are simply reflections off particles of dust, they do not appear on every picture taken in the same area by the same camera. If one is dealing with a natural phenomenon, such as dust or flying insects, orbs should be ubiquitous, but they are not. Also, it does not explain why they so frequently appear on photos taken at "haunted sites," but so seldom appear on ordinary photos taken under similar circumstances. Most readers have probably seen literally thousands of photos over the years shot under all kinds of lighting conditions, both indoor and out, without ever seeing an orb or other inexplicable reflection, so the fact that they seem to most frequently appear on photos taken at haunted locations must be considered at least interesting.

Finally, there are others who are quick to point out that "true" orbs do not reflect light the same way a dust particle or flying insect does, but are instead generally more opaque and, in some cases, even appear to have rings within them. Additionally, some that have appeared on video cameras are occasionally seen to abruptly change direction or make other unnatural movements that would seem to argue against them being natural objects. That doesn't prove they are paranormal energies, of course, but it implies that the light refraction theory doesn't seem to go far enough in explaining all of these anomalies with any degree of thoroughness.

Vortexes[19]

Somewhat less common than orbs but similar in nature are those little clouds or spiraling wisps of light that sometimes appear in photos known as vortexes (or, sometimes, vortices). Usually appearing as a swirling spiral of light (though they can also be more substantive as well, sometimes taking on the form of an apparently opaque shape, often of considerable size), they, like their cousin the orb, are also thought to be spiritual energies in the process of manifesting themselves, but ones that are closer to achieving that goal than are their spherical cousins. In other words, a vortex can be thought of as an orb that is in the process of moving outside the confines of its energy bubble in an effort to take on a more human-like form.[20]

---

19. Sometimes also known as ectoplasmic energy or ectomist, I prefer the more general term "vortex" for these phenomena, both because it is more generic and due to the bad press words like ectoplasma have acquired over the years. Additionally, "vortex" is also sometimes used as a term to denote a passageway or doorway between the physical and spiritual realms or an area of particularly ubiquitous paranormal activity, though for this study it is meant exclusively in the context of a manifestation of energy similar to an orb.

20. Some, however, believe precisely the opposite: that the orb is the more advanced manifestation, with the vortex being the more primitive manifestation. Unfortunately, there is probably no way to determine which is correct.

Like orbs, vortexes too are usually dismissed as reflections of light off either exhaled breath or cigarette smoke, with the more substantive opaque shapes being explained away as camera straps or some other object that has inadvertently fallen in front of the lens (human hair, for example, makes for especially "spooky" vortexes). Again, like the "orbs as dust" theory, this explanation probably does account for the majority of vortexes caught on film (especially those taken by amateurs. It is easy to forget about objects inadvertently placed in front of a camera lens and then enthusiastically proclaim the resultant anomaly a "ghost," so this explanation does carry considerable weight).

However, vortexes have their defenders as well, who maintain that "true" vortexes look nothing at all like exhaled breath or cigarette smoke, but instead have an eerily unique and unusual pattern all their own. Additionally, they also point out that vortexes shot by careful investigators need to be taken seriously, since such people are usually meticulous about ensuring that camera straps are removed and people are not smoking in the vicinity at the time the photo is taken. Plus there are those vortexes that seem to be forming limbs and other recognizable human features to take into account. Though these can be the result of the eye wanting to bring order to a random swirl of mist (sometimes known as "matrixing"), some of the best vortex photos truly do appear inexplicable, so it would be unwise to dismiss all of them as simply tricks of the eye or as the results of ham-handed incompetence.

Full Body Manifestations (FBMs)

The "holy grail" of all spirit photos is the rare full body manifestation (sometimes also referred to as the full torso apparition). These are images in which an entity appears either partially or fully formed and recognizable as a human being (or, sometimes, an animal). Though commonly transparent and ill-defined, in some rare cases, they may appear completely opaque and solid and, since the figure is usually clear enough to be readily identifiable by the deceased's friends or

Common Photo Anomalies
Frequently Mistaken for Ghosts

What is often mistaken for a ghostly haze (commonly known as a vortex) is often nothing more than exhaled breath or cigarette smoke. The imagination then finds identifiable shapes where none actually exist. (See if you can pick out the face in the photo. Hint: left center.)

More solid-looking vortexes are usually camera straps or other objects that have inadvertently fallen in front of the lens. Notice how the flash makes it appear even more "ghostly."

Lens flares and dust, rain, snow, or even insects are frequently mistaken for balls of ectoplasmic energy commonly referred to as orbs. This is a significant problem when shooting photos in dusty, dark places (especially at night when the flash may reflect off almost any object).

family, FBMs are especially valuable evidence of both paranormal activity and postmortem existence.

Full body manifestations often appear quite unexpectedly in photos, most commonly in the background or in the periphery of an image. In some of the more remarkable examples, they can even appear to be posing for the camera, just as a person would do in life. There are even a number of instances where the image of a dead soldier or airman appears in a group photo standing alongside his still living mates, as if he is unaware or unwilling to accept his own death or refuses to break those close bonds that often exist among men who have been through combat together. It is almost as if they are intent on continuing to carry on much the same way they did during life and will even smile for the camera alongside their corporeal colleagues. As such, while it certainly seems that some ghosts are quite aware they are being photographed, there is no way of knowing whether this is true of all ghosts, for there are those apparitions that seem to be completely oblivious to the camera and appear to have been caught by accident.

There are only about a dozen really superb full body manifestation photos in existence, and these constitute some of the best evidence of paranormal phenomenon on record. However, as I said earlier, they will never constitute proof of ghosts simply because even the very best spirit photos are capable of being hoaxed. While they are tantalizing tastes of what sophisticated equipment might be capable of recording, they seem forever fated to remain just outside the realm of empirical evidence. That's not to say that one day a few seconds of clear, crisp color footage of a full-bodied apparition walking down a stairway in front of a room full of witnesses may not earn a very serious look; it's just that scientific standards of what constitutes proof are unlikely to ever be met by a bit of flickering celluloid or an image imprinted on magnetic tape, no matter how convincing it might be. Yet this does not prevent the investigator from trying, however, nor will it likely stand as a roadblock to attempting to photograph paranormal activity in the future.

Types of Cameras and Other Photographic Devices

Having looked briefly at the history and mechanics of photographing ghosts, it is necessary to more closely examine the technology available to the modern-day ghost hunter in his or her quest. Not surprisingly, there is a plethora of cameras available to the serious paranormal investigator today, and each has its own capabilities and limitations. We will briefly examine each type of device in turn to determine what those strengths and weaknesses might be.

Film Camera

The oldest and, in many cases, most reliable type of camera used today, the traditional negative-producing 35mm camera still offers the best final product, due entirely to its high resolution capability and the fact that it provides one with a film negative that can be used to blow up a particular image while still retaining a high degree of definition. It is also far more difficult to alter a negative than manipulate a print (though not impossible. It does, however, require some technical prowess) thereby giving a negative that can get by the experts a better than average pedigree.

However, they are not without their flaws and limitations. Old or partially exposed film can produce all types of anomalies that can be mistaken by the novice for a ghostly manifestation, and double exposures are always a problem (though this is quickly becoming less so with the advent of self-winding cameras). Heat and excessive cold can also affect film, while airborne particles, poor weather conditions, bad lighting, and a host of other circumstances can result in unusual objects appearing on a negative that might easily be misidentified as a ghostly image. Even something as prosaic as a camera strap or an insect flying in front of the lens can later be identified as an "orb" or "vortex," so there is much that can go wrong with standard film cameras as well (as is true with all cameras, for that matter). Finally, there is an additional disadvantage in using standard print film: time and money. Throughout the course of a single evening's investigation, ghost hunters will often shoot dozens of rolls of film in an effort to capture an image of a ghost, resulting in development costs that can become substantial over the long run (unless they are capable of developing the film themselves). Film can also be difficult to load (especially in a darkened room or outdoors) and it also has a disadvantage in that it forces the investigators to wait until the film has been developed to determine if they recorded anything of interest, by which time paranormal activity at the haunted location may have waned. For the most part, however, the film camera, when in competent hands, remains among the most valuable of all the tools in the investigator's arsenal.

Instant Cameras

When Polaroid introduced the instant camera back in the 1960s, it proved to be a boon to ghost hunters, for now they did not need to wait days for a roll of film to be developed, but could see the fruits of their labor appear before their eyes in a matter of minutes. This resulted in a number of very impressive spirit photos being produced over the years, resulting in the instant camera remaining an uncommon but still valuable ghost-hunting tool even today.[21]

The biggest advantage of the instant camera, other than the savings it presents in terms of time and expense, is that it permits the anomaly to develop on film before multiple witnesses, thus greatly diminishing the chance of trickery and largely eliminating the likelihood of developing errors. Additionally, since there is no negative, it also eliminates the chance that someone has manipulated a photo, and, as each photo is immediately ejected upon being taken, it is impossible to produce a double exposure, thereby eliminating another common explanation for ghostly images appearing unexpectedly in a photo.

The drawbacks of instant cameras are basically that they will not generally produce as clear or crisp a picture as a 35mm camera, and

---

21. With the advent of the digital camera, both Polaroid and Kodak have stopped manufacturing instant cameras, making their continued use in the future increasingly problematic.

the fact that they lack negatives makes it almost impossible to make clear reproductions or enlargements (to do so involves either scanning the original or taking a photo of the photo, usually causing serious degradation in the process and so reducing the overall image quality). Additionally, they also suffer from the same problems as a traditional film camera in terms of dust, flying insects, and other objects being mistaken for ghostly manifestations. And, of course, instant film can go bad as well (though the results are usually more pronounced and obvious), so the same precautions need to be taken with the instant camera as would be required with any camera.

Digital Cameras

The advent of digital cameras revolutionized the ghost-hunting trade, for suddenly it gave investigators the ability to shoot an almost unlimited number of photos that could be examined on the spot to determine if any ghostly images might be present. They also eliminated the possibility of double exposures and the difficulty of changing film quickly in poor light, and saved the researcher time by eliminating the waiting period between shooting and developing the film. This made ghost hunting quick, easy, and almost universally affordable, and overnight the ranks of camera-toting ghost-hunting enthusiasts swelled. As such, the vast majority of spirit photos that have come out over the last decade have been taken with digital cameras, accounting for the vast profusion of such photos appearing on web sites and creating something of a renaissance in the ghost photo industry.

There is no doubt digital cameras offer certain advantages film cameras cannot match, but unfortunately their disadvantages often offset their usefulness as a paranormal investigative tool. The biggest problem is that, like the instant cameras, they also do not produce negatives but exist purely as dots of color (known as pixels) on an electronic medium which, when blow up, becomes increasingly diffused until, in extreme close-ups, the image loses all definition and detail, making it difficult to determine anything useful from the image. Even newer, higher resolution cameras—while definitely better than the more common lower-end digitals—still lose definition when enlarged, making ghost photos taken with a digital camera problematic at best. Digital photos also can be brought into various photo manipulation programs and electronically altered and, since they have no negative with which to compare the altered version, no record exists to document the changes, thereby making the photo almost worthless as evidence. Though high resolution digital photos may still be capable of capturing valid evidence within their electronic matrix, even the best pictures will remain tainted by the medium's capability and limitations. As such, while a few investigators like to use them because of a belief they can record images on a higher light spectrum than can film cameras, most use them only for documenting a location or for taking preliminary shots to determine possible paranormal activity prior to using a film camera.

Infrared Film Cameras

Some of the more sophisticated paranormal investigators have taken to using infrared film in the belief that spiritual energies might well be visible in this light range and, since a ghostly image captured through such a process should be less prone to trickery, the photo should carry more weight as evidence of paranormal activity than regular film. However, this presumes such energies do, in fact, manifest themselves in the infrared wavelength, which begs the question of how a ghost can be captured on both infrared and regular cameras if they exist primarily in these lower light spectrums. Yet, if we are dealing with the unknown, the theory that ghosts might be more readily apparent in one light frequency than in another should be no more remarkable than the fact they can occasionally be seen at all.

The biggest problem with infrared imaging is both production costs and the difficulty in using the film. It is not something any novice can readily pick up, and it can be a very difficult medium to master, making it a tool for only the most determined and skillful investigator—but one that should prove increasingly popular as they become easier to operate and cheaper to purchase in the future.

3-D Cameras

This is a powerful tool that can yield some compelling evidence in the right hands. It works by capturing an image from more than one angle (as a regular film or digital camera does), thereby giving the object in question some spatial dimension. This partially eliminates dust, moisture, or the insertion of an object in front of the lens as an explanation for an anomaly, since the object is seen from different perspectives simultaneously, giving it a sense of existing within a three-dimensional context and so making identifying the source easier. This also makes any object caught on a 3-D camera of particular interest, since fakery is so much more difficult (though not, of course, impossible).

3-D cameras, however, suffer from the same problems as any film camera in terms of expense, development costs and time, and transportability (they tend to be larger than most cameras and more ponderous, though they are coming down in size). As they become more accessible, however, they should start becoming a more valuable and common tool in the investigator's bag of tricks.

Video Cameras

Obviously, capturing a paranormal entity moving is better than a still image, for it demonstrates a "something" that is capable of interacting with the environment. As such, video cameras are becoming increasingly popular among investigators, particularly as their size and price have come down extensively over the years, making them both more affordable and easier to use. Further, the addition of microphones, and with it the possibility of capturing ghostly sounds, makes them even more useful as a ghost-hunting tool. It is not remarkable, then, that an increasing number of videos are appearing, making the case for ghosts even more compelling in some circles.

Yet they are not without their drawbacks as well. Like all cameras, they too can be tricked by light reflections off dust, flying insects, or water droplets and, with the clever manipulation of some Plexiglas and a few off-camera props, can be tricked into recording some extraordinary reflections that can appear quite convincing. There is also a well-documented tendency for video cameras (as is often true of all sophisticated electronic equipment) to consistently malfunction at a "haunting," sometimes rendering them useless at the most crucial moment.[22] Additionally, like any photographic medium, videotape is also susceptible to manipulation and careful editing, again compromising its usefulness in providing evidence of paranormal activity. Despite all these shortcomings, however, if ghosts are ever to produce some hard, visual evidence, it will probably come from this medium. Clear, color footage of a full body manifestation in good light and under controlled circumstances would likely constitute some of the best evidence possible of a ghost, making their continued use not only invaluable, but essential if ghosts are ever to be proven to science's demanding standards.

Thermal Imaging Cameras

A fairly new tool that has come on the market recently is the thermal imaging camera, a device that perceives images according to their heat signature rather than in their ability to reflect light, thus giving a person the ability to detect objects that might otherwise remain invisible to the naked eye. In doing so, they give the investigator a new and never-before-realized advantage: the ability to visibly detect heat anomalies within a space, which, since ghosts are frequently believed to generate cold spots during manifestation, cannot be underestimated.[23] The only drawback would seem to be that it can also capture naturally occurring vents and drafts as well, thus making it difficult to determine which is a natural phenomena and which is possibly indicative of ghostly activity. Plus, they have the advantage in that they can film in complete darkness, thereby largely eliminating the most common

---

22. This common tendency for electronic equipment to stop functioning at haunts has been attributed by some to entities pulling energy out of the environment and inadvertently draining batteries in the effort. It is an interesting possibility, but one that lacks any solid evidence to support it.

23. How and why a ghost creates a cold spot is a source of some debate. Some have suggested that in pulling energy from the environment, they reduce the number of molecules in the air and so lower the ambient temperature in a particular and measurable space, which should, at least as far as the higher–end thermal imaging cameras go, be visible.

photo anomalies such as lens flare, flash reflections off dust, and camera straps.

Though somewhat pricey and as such affordable only to better financed investigators, its value in detecting paranormal activity in the future can only be guessed at, but it has the potential to, if not revolutionize, at least bring tremendous strides to the entire field of paranormal research.

Exploring Other Ghost-Hunting Devices: The Exciting World of the EVP

Cameras, while traditional and valuable tools in the ongoing effort at securing evidence of ghosts, are only one method of many available to the paranormal investigator. While a photograph certainly is a valuable piece of evidence of ghostly activity, it is by no means always the most valuable or even the most interesting type of evidence out there. Perhaps of all the equipment used by modern investigators, one of the more intriguing and exciting is also one of the most simple to use: the good old-fashioned tape recorder.

Most people assume ghosts are something one sees, not hears, so many are surprised to learn that some entities actually produce sounds and that, on occasion, these sounds have been captured on tape. As such, the tape recorder has become another valuable tool in the ghost hunter's bag of tricks (especially as higher quality, ultrasensitive microphones have become increasingly available and affordable) and one that is beginning to rival the camera as an effective means of proving the existence of the paranormal. This has made it an increasingly useful and reasonably inexpensive tool that no real investigator should be without.

Auditory recordings of ghosts are known in the trade as electronic voice phenomenon (EVPs) and, while a comparatively new phenomenon, EVPs have provided some intriguing and compelling evidence for the existence of ghosts. Of course, how a spiritual energy might manifest sound waves is a mystery, but then one no more inexplicable than trying to understand how a ghost can appear to the naked eye or on film without a physical body. It seems the one should be no more or less remarkable—or likely—than the other, so the idea that a ghost might "talk" needs to be seriously considered. (This is especially true in light of a number of very interesting examples of EVPs that have been obtained over the years). Not only have inexplicable sounds, such as scratching, rapping, scraping, or other odd or "out-of-place" sounds been captured, but even fully identifiable and understandable voices have been occasionally heard on tape. What is curious is that frequently these sounds are not heard at the time they are recorded, but only on later playback. At least in that respect then, EVPs share with ghost photos the tendency that an entity usually is not apparent to the observer at the time, requiring investigators to be as patient and persistent in their efforts at capturing disembodied voices on tape as they must be to capture an image on film.

There are generally two methods investigators use in their efforts at capturing an EVP. In the first, known as the *passive method*, a high-quality tape recorder with an extremely powerful microphone is placed inside a closed, sealed room where paranormal activity is thought to be occurring[24] and left to run by itself. Then, once finished, the tape is rewound, the volume turned to its highest setting, and the investigator simply listens for any unusual sounds that might occur. The other method, known as the *active method*, also makes use of a high-quality recorder, but in this case a subject asks a string of questions into the air (much as one would in a séance) at ten- or fifteen-second intervals,[25] after which the tape is rewound and played back at full volume later. If successful, the investigator might hear a voice in the background responding to their questions or, in the case of the

---

24. Careful investigators take great steps to ensure a closed room where EVP recordings are being taken is not entered while the recording is going on, even to the point of putting flour on the floor to determine the presence of footprints. Even the smallest breach of discipline can render an entire recording worthless.

25. This second technique has generally proven more successful as it seems to encourage ghostly interaction more than does simply waiting for a ghost to say something of its own accord. Both methods, however, have produced some impressive results.

passive method, a cacophony of unidentified sounds or even a muffled conversation might be captured. Normally, of course, just as dozens of rolls of film shot at a paranormal "hot spot" usually come up empty, most investigators are left with either hours of uninterrupted silence or explainable noises, such as running furnaces or water moving through pipes. Frequently, however, unexplained popping or scratching sounds can be heard, and occasionally a discernible voice (or voices) can be made out—often weakly—in the background, (though sometimes these voices have been clear and distinct enough to be understandable to the point that entire coherent sentences have been recorded). However, the investigator needs to be especially careful here, for the brain dislikes random patterns of noise and often attempts to make sense of even the most indistinct gibberish. As such, investigators need to be careful they are not hearing what they "believe" an EVP is saying rather than letting the recording speak for itself. Just as people used to play old Beatles records backward in an effort to hear the "secret encoded clues" that implied lead singer Paul McCartney was dead (he wasn't), so too are humans quite capable of fooling themselves into hearing intelligible phrases where none exists. Additionally, there is also the problem that sound can travel remarkable distances under the proper circumstances, meaning that muffled voices may not be a ghostly message at all, but a fully corporeal conversation taking place in another room some distance away. As such, the investigators need to be very careful about the location and the acoustical patterns inherent to the locale in which they record, lest they inadvertently pick up distant sounds and misinterpret them to be paranormal in nature.

Other Gadgets No Serious Ghost Hunter Should Be Without

Beyond visually or audibly detecting a ghost, there are several other ways to determine if one is supposedly in the presence of a paranormal entity, most of which make use of highly sensitive electronic devices of various descriptions, all designed to measure changes in the electromagnetic field or air temperature. What makes these devices especially useful in determining potential paranormal activity is not only the fact that they are far less prone to trickery, but that they tend to provide data that carries a bit more weight with science than do blurry photos and indiscernible background noises. While they have their drawbacks and limitations, especially in the hands of the incompetent and inexperienced, as a rule they are more trustworthy than either human memory or "feelings" and can do much in demonstrating that one has indeed found something "strange in the neighborhood" (to quote a line from the *Ghostbusters* theme song).

EMF Meter

Since it is theorized that ghosts are basically collections of ambient energy, and since all energy puts out an electromagnetic signature, it is logical to imagine that a ghost might register on any instrument designed specifically to detect such energy. As such, electro-magnetic field (EMF) meters are standard fare for all ghost hunters and an invaluable tool in determining when "something" has entered the room so cameras can be pointed and tape recorders turned on.

EMF meters are used in one of two ways. Like tape recorders, they can be used in both active and passive modes. In the active mode, the investigators carry the meter with them and take readings at various points throughout a location until they encounter a reading that is dramatically different from the previously recorded baseline readings and has no obvious electromagnetic source to account for it (such as electrical conduit or an electronic device being turned on). Such a reading, while hardly proof of the presence of a ghost, would be evidence that there is some inexplicable source of electromagnetic energy present, and that could be indicative of a paranormal presence. In the passive mode, remote EMF sensors are placed throughout a locale and tied into a central computer from which an entire structure can be monitored simultaneously. In this case, what the investigator is looking for is not simply a change in the electromagnetic readings in a particular room, but a sequence of such changes moving in an obvious pattern, possibly indicating a paranormal presence on the move.

Of course, EMF meters cannot really tell whether a ghost has entered a room. All they can tell you is that there is a change in the electromagnetic energy in a particular space, not what is causing it, and since electromagnetic energy exists almost everywhere in nature (all electrical appliances, especially microwaves, computers, and televisions—along with Earth itself—emit considerable amounts of the stuff all the time), one would be presumptuous to assume that any spike in an EMF reading is evidence that a ghost is making a visit. There are simply too many other naturally occurring sources of energy that might account for the unusual reading.

However, it can tell you that *something* unusual is happening, especially if the readings are suddenly inconsistent with the baseline readings that were taken beforehand, and there is no readily apparent electrical source to explain the sudden change. Like all energy-sensing equipment, however, it will never be more than a helpful tool for finding a ghost and has only limited value as an empirical source of evidence. It can be extremely useful, however, especially when used in conjunction with other devices, for an EMF spike recorded at the precise moment an orb or vortex appears on film, for example, would give the photo considerably more weight than it would have otherwise.

Ion Counter

Some paranormal investigators believe ghosts are comprised of highly charged ions, and so, like the EMF meter, an ion counter can also be a useful tool for detecting the possible presence of paranormal activity. It also has the advantage in that, unlike electromagnetic energy, clusters of ionic energy are less common occurrences in nature, making an anomalous reading more inexplicable and so potentially more useful. The downside, however, is that such instruments are difficult to use and, as such, are not as common. They also suffer, as do all electronic devices, from being only as valuable as the user's level of competency. It takes considerable time and effort to learn how to read an ion meter correctly, and so it is only useful when in the hands of an experienced and scientifically knowledgeable user. However, if used properly, like its more common cousin, the EMF meter, it can be extremely useful in highlighting potential paranormal activity and so is extremely helpful in the ghost hunter's quest.

Thermometer

Most people are familiar with the famous "cold spots" of horror movies, when a ghost supposedly signals its presence through a quick drop in room temperature (which turns out to be one of the few elements of a haunting Hollywood has gotten right, though they tend to overdo it). As such, since paranormal activity is often associated with sudden and dramatic drops in localized temperature, it follows that a sensitive and precise handheld point-and-shoot thermometer would be extremely useful.

The obvious problem with such a device, of course, is that users must be especially careful that they are not picking up some naturally occurring draft and, even more so, that they are using the instrument correctly. Skeptics have repeatedly demonstrated how easy it is to get erroneous readings off even the best devices, forcing the investigator to be extremely careful when using such equipment, while understanding why it is important to get multiple readings from different angles (and duplicate devices) before jumping to any conclusions. Also, it should be remembered that even if an unexplained cold spot is identified, there is no guarantee that anyone will see or hear—much less photograph—anything out of the ordinary. Like the EMF meter and the ion counter, it is only one more tool that tells the investigator something might be present, not proof that it is.

Motion Detectors

If ghosts are made up of invisible energy, it is difficult to see how one might acquire enough mass to set off a motion detector. A ghost should, one would imagine, be no more capable of doing so than a flashlight beam or a gentle breeze. However, as we know so little about what a ghost is made of in the first place, the possibility that one might register on a motion detector under certain circumstances must be at least entertained. Additionally, since a few investigators have reported some success using such devices, they remain an often important tool in the ghost hunter's arsenal and are likely to remain so in the future.

Even if they are not capable of being tripped by a ghost, however, motion detectors can still provide other useful information. For example, they often prove helpful in detecting poltergeist activity, for while they may not be able to pick up a ghost, they can detect objects a ghost might hurtle across the room, making it possible to thoroughly stake out an entire locale with relative ease. If nothing else, they are at least useful for ensuring that no unauthorized person enters a sealed room and have even been found helpful in locating hidden animals that have subsequently been held responsible for some of the inexplicable "ghostly" noises people have been hearing. As such, motion detectors remain, if nothing else, useful as a security measure and a tool for explaining inexplicable noises.

Night Vision Goggles

Ever since these devices first hit the market a few years ago, they have become extremely popular with ghost hunters, many of whom are quick to turn out the lights at a potential haunted site and spend the evening wandering about studying the world through these remarkable devices.

However, it remains to be seen just how useful a device they really are in attempting to see an invisible being. If ghosts are essentially invisible, they should be no more apparent through a star scope than they would be to the naked eye. In fact, since ghosts appear to be able to reflect light, they should theoretically be more visible in a lighted room than in a darkened one, thereby rendering such devices less valuable than one might imagine. As such, while night vision goggles might be helpful in staking out an unlighted locale (such as a cemetery or old barn), it is difficult to see how useful they might be beyond that. While they might prove useful in determining whether any fully corporeal beings are wandering about in the dark trying to fool investigators, for the most part night vision devices appear to be a better tool for the Bigfoot hunter than the ghost hunter, although that is simply an opinion.

As a sidebar, this brings up the entire issue of why some ghost hunters (and especially those shown on television programs) prefer to turn the lights out throughout a location when attempting to find evidence of paranormal activity. It strikes me as being not only potentially more physically dangerous to the investigator, but since most ghost sightings take place in lighted rooms (and often in broad daylight), it doesn't make sense that ghosts are more likely to appear in a dark room or that they are primarily nocturnal in nature. As such, the point of looking for ghosts in the dark appears illogical and even unwise, especially when one considers how much easier it is to let one's imagination get the best of them in a darkened room than in a well-lit one, thereby potentially reducing the quality and credibility of any paranormal occurrence. While some contend that turning off all electrical devices may be helpful in reducing the electromagnetic signature throughout a location, thereby improving the chance of locating a potential ghost on an EMF meter, that too seems a stretch. Paranormal activity can be seen on an EMF meter regardless of whether a location has is lighted or not, *as long as good baseline readings were taken initially.* The EMF meter reads fluctuations to these baseline readings, so it doesn't matter whether the sweeps are done in the dark or not. It's simply a comparison with what was initially recorded. Additionally, if ghosts feed off ambient electrical energy, it might actually be helpful to keep the power on to provide them at least a potential source of energy from which to manifest. Turning off the power, then, might actually be detrimental to getting a ghost to appear, explaining why those who commonly use the technique of "going dark" often have such dismal results; they're actually starving their paranormal visitors of the very power they require to manifest at the precise moment they need it the most.

As such, while turning unnecessary lights off and reducing power output might be helpful in reducing the noise level within a haunted locale (thus improving the possibility of getting clearer EVPs and hearing poltergeist activity), and while it would probably be wise to turn off major sources of noise and distraction such as television sets, radios, and computers while staking out a location, for the most part it seems at least some lighting would be preferable for ghost hunting so events can be clearly seen, trickery made more difficult, and any paranormal activity more clearly documented.

Conclusion

There are other devices the ghost hunter sometimes uses, though these are more controversial and, in some cases, bizarre. Beyond the occasional Geiger counter (are ghosts radioactive?) and compass (the poor man's EMF meter), there are those who use everything from Ouija boards to candles and divining rods to locate or entice their otherworldly guests into making an appearance. How useful such devices are is a matter of both personal opinion and considerable debate, but all of this should be enough to demonstrate that the art of ghost hunting is nothing if not thorough. Whether any of these tools will eventually prove successful in convincing the scientific community of the existence of ghosts is unknown, but that there are dedicated men and women out there that spend many a night staking out and waiting for a manifestation to appear is a tribute to their determination and patience.

The reader will also notice I have omitted one of the most common tools of ghost hunting, and that is the services of the professional medium or psychic. This is intentional, but in no way is it intended as a slight against those men and women who perform this service. I omit them simply because their value as determinants in the paranormal quest is purely subjective and largely beyond the ability to test or quantify (in other words, they do not produce "hard" evidence the way mechanical devices do). Unlike a film negative or an EMF reading, there is no way to gage the accuracy of a medium to determine whether an entity is actually in residence, and so they must always remain just outside the venue of being considered empirically acquired data. This does not diminish their value in the search, of course, but it is my opinion that any information they might provide is going to be incidental at best and certainly will do little to either scientifically confirm or disprove the existence of a ghost. Yet I recognize and appreciate their efforts and remain convinced a medium can be a valuable supplemental resource to any ghost hunt and may ultimately prove indispensable in the future as the science of the supernatural takes on momentum and opens itself to fresh ideas.

part three

Examining the "Dark Side" of Ghosts

Having earlier examined some reasons why a deceased individual might choose or, perhaps, be compelled to remain on the earthly plane, it is next important to more closely examine one aspect of this topic that has profound implications to the study of ghosts and the paranormal in general, and that is the role of evil.

The New Age supposition that the spiritual realm is a place of unending joy and peace is just that: a supposition. However, if we are to remain consistent with the idea that consciousness not only survives death but is capable of existing within other contexts of reality, we must accept the notion that just as there are malevolent people in life, there are undoubtedly malevolent—or, if you prefer, "evil"—people in death. The old cliché that a leopard can't change its spots is true in this respect: if you leave this world as a negative personality, it seems a given that you will exist as such in the next world. Therefore, it is logical to assume that within the light there are a few dark blemishes out there that manage from time to time to make their presence known within our world of linear time and space. How they might do this is a source for debate, but if we allow for the idea that loving people can still interact with us after they have passed over, we must accept the idea that hateful ones can do the same. To permit the one allows the other; to disallow either eliminates both.

This is not a particularly popular idea, for the subject is already frightening enough to many people that dragging evil ghosts into the mix can be an especially uncomfortable tangent to consider. Yet if we are to do as complete and thorough a study as possible, it is necessary we consider this element of the equation as well. As such, in this section we will examine all the ramifications evil could have on the supernatural realm, and whether there is such a thing as "bad" ghosts or, even, potentially, demons. (We will look at the subject of demonic possession as well.) While such elements may seem an unnecessary digression, it may be far more important than some may think, for it is in understanding this aspect of the paranormal that we may inadvertently find the key to understanding ourselves and so be better prepared to deal with the dark side of humanity, be it in the flesh or in the spirit.

chapter eight

Malevolent Entities and Ghostly Parasites

To the best of my knowledge, I have interacted with a malevolent spirit only once in my life. As a twenty-one-year-old sailor living in San Diego, California, I believe I came into the presence of a "something" in my apartment one evening that was so decidedly evil that it was almost overpowering. I am not sure why I had the misfortune of encountering this entity; it may have had something to do with the fact that I had just recently converted to Christianity and was curious about how the spiritual realm worked and so could have inadvertently permitted this energy into my life. In any case, all I know is that for several nights this "presence" would enter my apartment and fill me with a sense of dread that was almost palpable for several minutes before leaving as abruptly as it had come.

Eventually deciding that I would have to confront this being if peace was ever to return, I finally found the courage to talk to it and insist that it leave permanently (actually, I "cast it out" by invoking the name of Jesus, just as I had been taught to do by my church). While initially this only seemed to make its energy stronger, eventually, as I kept up my homemade exorcism, it began to waver and, finally, dissipate. It returned once more, the very next evening, but this time its energy was far more subdued, and I, now endowed with a newfound sense of invincibility, again addressed it and invoked the name of Jesus until it finally left completely and vanished, never to return again. It was gone as completely as if it had never appeared and I had no more encounters with it, nor have I had any similar experiences since.

Some might suggest I had simply imagined the whole thing. After all, I was young and presumably impressionable, and my newfound faith's teachings about demons may have had more influence on me than I'd imagined. (The fact that I did my best impression of an exorcist couldn't help but reinforce that idea.) However, while I do not deny that such has to be considered at least a possibility, I find it interesting that I had never encountered anything like it before, nor have I had such an experience since despite holding onto a deeply held belief in demons for years afterward. It seems that if I was a victim of some religious-induced hysteria or the power of suggestion, I should have had multiple encounters with my fantasy opponent throughout the years, leaving me to wonder why my imagination was so open to suggestion for only those few weeks over twenty-five years ago.

The one thing I could not deny, however, was the very strong feelings it invoked in me. I neither saw nor heard anything, but the negative energy it put off was as real as a cold drizzle, and I felt it on a very deep level. Had I truly encountered a demon or some other denizen of hell in my apartment all those years ago, or was it something else? If so, what did it want and, further, why did it leave when I told it to? I may never know the answers to these questions, but it did at least convince me that there is a side to the supernatural that is not so nice.

Since then I have learned a few things about these dark energies and am convinced that they can be dangerous—at least to the emotionally immature and psychologically unstable—and so must be taken seriously. After all, if there really are such entities in existence, it is important we not only acknowledge that fact but learn to deal with them in a constructive way. But before we can do that, we have to ask the basic question of whether there really could be such a thing as entities—both personalities and extra-celestials—that are so composed of negative energy that they feed off fear the way a plant feeds on nutrients in the soil, and, if so, are they dangerous to us here in the physical realm? For that matter, do evil people commonly (or even automatically) become ghosts, and, if so, how do they affect us here in the physical realm?

Malevolent Entities

It has always been my contention that if the human personality does survive death, it does so largely intact and still in possession of its primary traits, temperament, and energy. As such, we must be open to the probability that there are such things as malevolent or "dark" personalities and work from that premise. Unfortunately, when most people think of such entities, that usually conjures up images of horned imps or some other Hollywood-induced monstrosity, but I am suggesting no such thing. We will deal specifically with the issue of demons later, but for now we will confine our discussion to the area of malevolent human entities or what I like to refer to as dark personalities, and examine a few ideas about how such beings might affect the living and to what degree.

Before we move on, however, it is first important to better understand just what it is we are talking about here. In chapter four we briefly looked at the concept of an angry ghost—a personality that is so full of anger and the thirst for revenge that it essentially traps itself on the Earth plane for decades or even centuries at a time—but that's not what I'm suggesting here. An angry ghost is not necessarily an evil ghost, nor is an evil ghost necessarily angry. An angry ghost is a human personality that is stuck on the Earth plane by its own rage and resentment. An evil ghost, in contrast, is more akin to a criminally insane or destructive ego that enjoys doing evil purely for the sake of being evil. It is further differentiated from an angry ghost in that it is truly sick and not merely jealous, upset, hurt, or frustrated (though, of course, it may be these things as well). It is a far more unique manifestation and one that we need to look at in more detail, both in an attempt to acquire as complete an understanding of the paranormal realm as possible, and in an effort to protect ourselves from what could be a potentially dangerous aspect of that realm as well. To do that, however, will require that we consider precisely in what way such entities are dangerous to us in the flesh and, even more importantly, to what extent they can harm us. For example, are they capable of doing physical harm or even, perhaps, of affecting our free will and coercing us into doing things we might not otherwise normally do?

To begin with, it is probable that such entities interact within our world in much the same way normal or mischievous personalities might, in that they attempt to pull enough energy from the environment to manifest or, at a minimum, interact with material objects in some way. As such, some poltergeist manifestations might well be the work of malevolent spirits (although it is more likely most such activity is the work of mischievous or playful ghosts rather than evil ones). In effect, then, "bad" ghosts are not much different from regular ghosts in the way they function, and they probably retain many of the same capabilities and limitations as do their less disturbed colleagues.

However, since negative energy carries a different signature than does positive or neutral energy, the malevolent ghost generally makes itself known in a different way than does a "regular" ghost. Whereas a traditional personality may put off an air of confusion, sadness, or even fear, the malevolent energy signals its presence by infecting a physical location with an overwhelming sense of dread, which usually gives one the feeling of being in the presence of something dark and evil. While frequently this is the extent of its power, sometimes it may manifest itself in more substantial and dangerous ways. Cases of people being slapped or having their hair pulled by some unseen entity have been recorded, and even instances of scratch marks appearing spontaneously on a person's body—particularly on the arms and back—have been witnessed and, on a few occasions, even videotaped, thus implying that these entities are just as capable of and willing to manifest themselves within our realm as any other personality. Fortunately such encounters are relatively rare, but the fact that they occur at all should demonstrate that the power of evil and its resultant negative energy can be almost as powerful a force as love and the positive energy it produces, giving even the most seasoned paranormal investigator reason to tread carefully.

Since such personalities would seem to be so dangerous, it stands to reason that they should be doing tremendous damage all the time, but this does not seem to be the case. Instead, they appear to be extremely limited in what they can do, suggesting that there may well be some spiritual mechanism in place to restrain them. In essence, they may simply be restricted from interacting with the physical world by other policing entities unless we invite them, either directly or inadvertently, to do so.

One thing that does seem to be evident with negative energy, however, is that it seems to be attracted by the same. As such, locations that have been the scene of consistent and repeated acts of brutality and torture (such as abandoned prisons, for example) often seem to attract such entities. There is also some evidence that people who give off considerable amounts of negative energy themselves are capable of attracting them, much the way food left out in the open forest will eventually attract bears. As such, people who are by their very nature extremely negative, consistently angry or hostile, and generally hateful or suspicious of others might be good candidates to attract a malevolent entity, thus inadvertently "inviting" it into their life in some way.

Since accounts of genuinely evil ghosts are apparently rare, it may be that they express themselves in more subtle and less obvious ways. Attaching themselves to an especially suggestible or malicious psyche may even be a dark personality's preferred method of operation. Such influence, it might be argued, could well be the energy that fuels the most egregious acts of violence that occasionally manifest themselves within our society. Mass murderers and serial killers, for example, might be just two manifestations of such a "joining" (though, of course, evil influences may not always be the case. There are, after all, individuals out there who seem quite capable of committing atrocities without supernatural assistance).[26] The point is that if malevolent personalities really want to engage in evil, they could do so much more effectively from within the context of the human psyche than through more crude external efforts, perhaps making them more common within our world than we know.

How a malevolent spirit might achieve this "joining" is, of course, unknown, nor is there any way of knowing to what extent it can affect a highly suggestible human host. Yet even if we do not understand precisely how it might do this, it is not beyond reason to suppose that an especially strong-willed entity might be able to powerfully affect the right person under certain circumstances. How they might do this remains largely speculative, of course, but most likely all disembodied energies possess some ability to communicate telepathically and, as such, may be able to transfer their own thoughts onto an especially susceptible person. It might even work along the lines of a subliminal suggestion—one, however, that is strong and persistent enough to impact or even override a person's own thought processes. In effect, when the entity finds a suitable host and attempts to join with it, individuals so affected might suddenly begin developing thoughts of anger and violence—thoughts that they believe to be originating within themselves but are, in fact, of foreign origin.

Unfortunately, this sounds a lot like possession, but that's not what I'm talking about in this case. Possession—a subject we will examine more completely in chapter ten—is when an individual has been so completely co-opted by some external force that they lose all sense of free will and, in effect, becomes little more than a vessel that the evil entity uses to give itself animation. In this situation, however, the "host" or victim of this event still retains the power to choose whether or not to act on the evil impulses coursing through them; the entity is merely feeding its subject thoughts and ideas (or simply reinforcing

---

26. This is not to suggest that criminals should not be held responsible for their actions even if they are being influenced by some external entity. It is not a full-blown possession, after all, but more of a subtle energy that may influence but not override one's free will, making the criminal still fully accountable for their crime.

and encouraging those evil thoughts already resident within the subject's psyche) but it has no ability to force them to take any action whatsoever. In effect, it is more like an evil influence or "joining" than a genuine possession, with the subject free to ignore or even expel the evil influence at any time. The fact that they frequently choose not to do so and instead act on those evil impulses is more a reflection of the subject's spiritual and emotional state than it is an example of the entity's power. In effect, the entity is simply the fuse that ignites the gunpowder; it is the subject that brings all the explosives and chooses when and if to light the fuse at all.

The "Dark" Agenda

Even if we are prepared to accept the possibility that malevolent ghosts may exist, the question that needs to be asked is if they are a part of our reality, what is it they want? What would drive a malevolent entity to attempt to harm us or those we love? What is their purpose, their plans, their "agenda"?

To answer this question we need only look at ourselves. What is it among human beings that causes a tiny minority of us to actively seek to destroy our fellow *Homo sapiens?* Is it simply greed or hubris or even the quest for power that drives the engines of evil, or is it something else?

I believe the real reason for such malevolence is fear.

As a student of history I came to realize early on that what drove the great dictators of history to murder and intimidate their way to the top in their quest for power, and then led many of them to continue to murder millions of their countrymen once they achieved that power was not evil for evil's sake, but something else entirely. What drove them to commit their barbaric acts was, in fact, unmitigated fear; fear of losing their power, fear that others were plotting against them (forcing them to frequently turn on their own family and closest colleagues), and even the fear of losing their own minds. It has been said, for example, that during the darkest days of the old Soviet regime, when literally thousands of citizens were being executed or sent into Siberian exile each day, Joseph Stalin was the only free man in all of Russia. Nothing, however, could be further from the truth. Stalin was, as were most Soviets of that era, as frightened as everyone else and was convinced that murder was the only way to remain safe. The security he sought, however, always remained just out of reach regardless of how many people he killed because the more he murdered, the more he feared. It was a vicious cycle from which only his own death could release him. Stalin, Hitler, Amin, Pol Pot, Hussein, all of them eliminated their enemies, both real and imagined, because they were afraid of them. Fear is what ran their lives. They had to destroy in order to survive. To not do evil, then, was to put their own survival at risk.

Could that be what drives malevolent spirits as well? Is it possible that these dark souls may simply be frightened spirits who have convinced themselves they must destroy in order to survive?

If true, it is difficult to imagine how they might accomplish the sort of damage they need to do to find the relief they thirst for, especially since in the end the human soul is both immortal and indestructible. They may influence and torment people, but they can never relieve their fear and terror, and so they perpetuate a never-ending, self-defeating cycle of negativity that can keep them in a self-imposed hell for eons. Fortunately, as I said earlier, I believe such entities are uncommon, and I think they are uncommon for two reasons: first, since genuinely evil people are rare, genuinely evil entities should be rare as well. For those who question this statement, consider all the people you have personally met in your life and then ask yourself how many of them would you consider genuinely "evil"? Not just dishonest or nasty or promiscuous or even violent, but full-fledged, irredeemably evil? I suppose much of how you choose to answer lies in how you define evil, but most likely, unless you maintain a very loose definition of the term or work in law enforcement or as a criminal psychologist, you probably cannot name a single person you know personally who is genuinely, bona fide evil. As such, we should not assume there are many such entities in the spirit realm who are genuinely evil as well.[27]

The second reason I believe such entities are uncommon is because, as I alluded earlier, I am convinced there are forces at work restraining such beings from the other side. In other words, there may be spiritual "cops" in existence whose job it is to steer the most malevolent energies clear of the physical plane until such time as they can be pulled out of their own darkness and rehabilitated. This is all purely conjecture, of course, but if the spiritual realm is a place of peace, love, and joy as taught, a truly malevolent energy should have a hard time either enduring such an environment or avoiding the inherent love that permeates it.

Finally, it should be remembered that malevolent energies probably have as difficult a time manifesting within the physical realm as all energies do for many of the same reasons. Manifesting into linear time and space may be extremely difficult for even positive energies to achieve; negative energies, working from a lesser frequency then, may have an even harder time of it. Perhaps that is why they need to be invited into a person's life in order to become apparent; their vibrational level is so low they cannot find the resources to manifest without the help of a human host.

In any case, even if they are not particularly dangerous to those who operate from the higher energies of love (which dark personalities may do their best to avoid), they are still capable of doing great damage and psychological harm, and so they should be avoided. That is why dabbling in the occult can be so dangerous: one never knows exactly what they might be dealing with and can never be entirely certain they are prepared for what they might encounter. Dark energies may be rare but they still exist and may only be awaiting an invitation, no matter how lightly made or innocently tendered, to make themselves known.

---

27. Of course, even if the number is as low as one in ten thousand souls, that still constitutes many millions of such entities, especially considering the total number of souls that may exist within the universe.

Conclusion

That evil exists is a fact, and that it can manifest itself within the realm of the physical world should not be discounted or ignored. How destructive these energies are undoubtedly depends on how much power we choose to permit them to have in our lives. For those primitive souls already bent toward evil, they may serve as a type of "malevolence amplifier," inducing them toward ever more despicable acts of wickedness. This may be the engine that drives the serial killer and the rapist; when caught most confess to a lack of control over their dark desires, and some have even claimed to be responding to voices that told them to act on their depraved passions. While some of this may be little more than feeble efforts at self-justification, how many such people may have been genuinely motivated by disembodied personalities? It is unlikely we will ever know for certain, since such information rarely becomes accessible to the public.

But even more important is the knowledge that while dark, fear-driven entities do exist, most people will never encounter one. New Age beliefs teach the existence of a spiritual realm of light and love and that is probably the truest reality of what awaits the soul when it leaves the physical realm; evil is simply a temporary and lesser energy that exists within the periphery of our senses, designed purely to showcase the magnificence of love, especially when contrasted with the dullness of evil. In the end, all souls—even the darkest among them—will be drawn back into the light, for that is all that finally exists within the realm of the absolute. The victory of light over darkness is already a reality, as it has been since the beginning; it is just that there are those few lost souls who need to find that out the hard way and so choose to walk a much more difficult path than the rest of us. It is all a part of the process. It is all a part of existence.

chapter nine

Demons: Fact, Faith, or Fallacy?

Having just covered the subject of malevolent personalities in some detail, many will naturally wonder what of the traditional belief in demons? Even if we are willing to accept the possibility that there is such a thing as evil ghosts, that doesn't necessarily preclude the possibility that there are other, even more dangerous, more malevolent, and more powerful beings in existence that we have come to label as demons. In fact, they seem an integral part of the discussion and an important element to look at, especially considering the profound impact such beings would have in our world, were they to exist. As such, this is as good a place as any to discuss the issue of demons and the devil in some detail, for it is an issue deserving of careful consideration.

Some may consider this as simply a case of splitting hairs. After all, if there are malevolent entities at all, what difference does it make if we call them simply evil entities or demons? Doesn't it all, in the end, come down to the same thing?

Not entirely. Evil ghosts and demons are very different things. Malevolent personalities are simply individuals who have been trapped on the earth plane through their own fear and confusion and, further, may be gotten rid of fairly easily. A demon, on the other hand, is more of a quasi-religious being that possesses far more power than simply the ability to frighten and intimidate. In fact, demons are a major element of our understanding of reality in that it touches upon the issues of good and evil we all contend with each day. Plus, they have religious connotations in that they serve as characters upon which all of eternity is played out. They are the great chess pieces in some cosmic game that shape our entire social gestalt and serve as the means by which billions of people across the planet understand the world around them. Therefore, the question of whether such entities truly exist is more than mere semantics or a point of theoretical discussion; instead, it strikes at the very heart of the nature of the universe itself and determines for us whether that universe is essentially benign or a place we should fear.

As such, the issue of whether demons exist is an important one to consider, especially considering the ramifications inherent to the question itself. After all, if there really are such things as demons, their existence would undoubtedly have a profound impact not only within the realm of time and space, but on a sociopolitical level as well. In fact, some have made precisely that claim; in effect, blaming many of the world's problems on the malicious works of these invisible super-natural entities. Wars, brutal dictatorships, repressive societies, even teenage suicide, drug abuse, and lawlessness have all been laid at the feet of Satan and his legions, making the question of whether such entities exist increasingly important.

So are there such things as demons, and, if so, what exactly are they? For the purpose of this study, it will be necessary to more precisely define what is meant by a "demon." Cultural beliefs vary as to what these beings are, but most consider them malevolent spiritual beings that have the ability to interact with the physical universe—usually in negative or destructive ways. Further, they are differentiated from "normal" ghosts in that they are not the spirits of deceased human beings, but are spiritual beings that have always existed in a noncorporeal state and, as such, have always remained just outside the periphery of the world of pure matter.

In much of Africa and Asia, however, as well as other parts of the world, demons are not necessarily perceived to be evil or even malev-olent—at least until they have been sufficiently provoked to anger. Instead, they are often seen as extremely powerful entities that provide some service or oversee some aspect of tribal survival (such as prosperity, fertility, or the weather) and, as such, have even been known to achieve the status of minor gods in their own right. Despite their great power, however, such entities are but one type of spirit among many that are thought to exist within the supernatural realm and are no more or less powerful than any other. As such, they can usually be kept at bay through rituals and ceremonies or by invoking more benevolent entities for protection, which is normally done by a tribal elder or shaman. Therefore, in many cultures demons are seen as a natural part of the environment and, while greatly respected, are not to be feared unless one has done something to earn their ire.

Western theology is more specific in its understanding of what a demon is. In Western thought, a demon is a type of angel, which is a supernatural entity originally created by God and designed specifically to interact within the physical realm to do the Creator's bidding. In the Bible and other religious texts, angels serve as everything from messengers of great joy, such as recounted in the Christmas story told in the Gospel of Luke, to personal investigators, such as recorded in the story of Sodom and Gomorrah as told in Genesis, to instruments of divine wrath and retribution as illustrated in the Passover story and recounted in the Book of Exodus. They are formidable beings of great strength who enthusiastically serve the Creator in a myriad of ways and are a major element of almost every Western religious tradition. Angels are even supposedly responsible for laying the foundation of some of the world's great faiths; an angel, for example, is said to have dictated the Koran to the prophet Muhammad, while another angel supposedly led Mormon founder Joseph Smith, Jr. to a series of golden plates upon which were inscribed the book of Mormon, thus launching an entirely new and unique sect within Christianity. A demon, then, is simply one of these powerful beings that effectively "went bad" and rebelled against God, only to be cast out of heaven for its treachery.

Angels, however, do not periodically fall from God's graces and become demons, but supposedly did so all at once, long before humanity had come to Earth and, possibly, even before the creation of the universe itself. According to tradition, demons were the byproduct of a rebellion led by the most powerful among them, a being originally known as Lucifer but more commonly referred to as Satan, which has resulted in a universe engaged in a spiritual war ever since, with continual battles being waged between the powers of light—God and his legions of angels on one side—and the powers of darkness—Satan and his band of followers on the other. Earth, unfortunately, is apparently "ground zero" in this struggle, which is what supposedly explains much of the perceived evil in the world. Not surprisingly, in a world where war, crime, and brutality are a common part of the human experience, the idea that we are living on a spiritual battlefield, with the armies of God and Satan locked in a millennia-old battle for dominance, rings true for many and so remains a major element of the religious beliefs of many people to this day.

Interestingly, this is not a fringe belief held to by fundamentalist religionists, but has been accepted as fact by some of the most sophisticated and intelligent men and women of the twentieth century. Two of my early literary and theological heroes were British writer and lay theologian C. S. Lewis (author of such masterpieces of Christian literature as *Mere Christianity*, the *Screwtape Letters*, the *Great Divorce*, and the *Narnia* trilogy) and American psychologist M. Scott Peck (author of the best-selling *The Road Less Traveled* and a number of other books on ethics and spirituality), both of whom believed in demons and accepted the existence of a literal devil as fact. Further, except within the more liberal branches of the world's great faiths, rare is the priest, pastor, or minister (or rabbi or imam, for that matter) who does not preach, teach, or otherwise believe in a literal devil and its army of followers. Of course, while such a belief is to be expected from the clergy, according to many polls more than half of all adults in this country, even among those who do not consider themselves especially religious or belong to any particular organized belief system, profess to believe in these creatures. As such, demons remain an integral element of the spiritual understanding of literally billions of people around the world and have so thoroughly ensconced themselves within the human psyche that it is hard to imagine religion without them.

The Case For and Against Demons

Simply because billions of people believe in demons, however, does not prove they exist. As I said, demons and Satan have been so thoroughly ingrained into our culture that many people are perfectly willing to accept their existence without encountering such a being personally or even, for that matter, really giving the matter any great thought at all. As such, I suppose the best place to start is in simply asking the question of whether it is even hypothetically possible that there could be such a thing as a "demon" (at least as understood in the classic Western sense) or a superpowerful being known as Satan.

This is no easy question to answer, especially since, at least on the surface, logic would seem to argue for the existence of such beings. After all, since supposedly nothing can exist without its opposite, it is not difficult to imagine a good and loving God having his opposite in the form of a being of darkness and hatred, whom we refer to as Satan. Additionally, if God has his legions of angels designated to do his bidding, it is also logical to imagine his counterpart, Satan, would have his similar legions of fallen angels as well and, further, that these entities might in fact be locked in a life-and-death struggle even to this day.

However, such a belief is based on a number of assumptions, the main one being the belief that God really did create a multitude of special spiritual entities specifically designed to serve him, an assumption that—despite being a major element of traditional religious belief for thousands of years—is ripe for challenge.

Did God create angels and, if so, for what purpose? Was it the need to be worshipped? Loved? Admired? Served?

The most common answer is that God created such beings as a means of interacting with his "sinful" creation, making them essentially intermediaries designed to do his bidding. This belief, however, creates more questions than it answers, especially when one considers the several occasions recounted in the Bible when God was perfectly capable of and willing to interact with humans without any angelic assistance at all.[28] Obviously, if God can visit his creation any time he so chooses, this begs the question of precisely what purpose the angels serve.

That is only one part of the equation that needs to be addressed, however. An even more important problem is if we allow that God "needed" angels for some reason, how is it that a supposedly all-knowing God would not have foreseen that an element of these creatures would later rebel and drag, at least according to the Book of Revelation,[29] a third of their numbers down with them (along with, by most accounts, a majority of humanity as well)? It seems a tremendous oversight on his part not to have anticipated such a possibility and built in some safeguards to prevent it. Such a dilemma leaves us in the uncomfortable position of forcing us to choose between a God that is either inept (or, at the very least, tragically shortsighted) or a God that was fully aware of the inevitable rebellion and did nothing to prevent it, neither of which seems consistent with the idea of a perfect, all-knowing deity. Additionally, the entire issue fails to address how evil could come about at all in a universe that originated from pure goodness in the first place. Wouldn't this be a case of bad fruit (rebellious angels) emerging from a good tree (God), completely in contradiction to Jesus' own words in John that such was impossible?[30]

Religionists counter this point by reminding us that in order for the angels to be truly free to love and serve God, it was necessary that he endow these beings with free will, thereby effectively tying his own hands when they rebelled. However, this answer fails to account for the entire problem. Free will, after all, is not synonymous with immortality. If God can create a freewill being from nothing, then why can't he just as easily destroy it if it goes "bad"? In effect, even if God did create

---

28. Genesis 3:8–19, Genesis 18, Genesis 32:24–30, Exodus 3:4–4:17, and elsewhere.

29. Revelation 12:4. Exact meaning of "a third of the stars" is uncertain, but is generally considered to be a reference to the fallen angels.

30. Matthew 7:16–20.

freewill creatures in an effort to acquire their affection and allegiance, why not simply destroy those that refused to serve him once they made the decision to rebel, a wise precaution especially considering how dangerous such beings would later prove to be if left to their own devices? The old tried-and-true response that God could not destroy them for then their decision to follow him would be based on the desire for survival rather than out of true, heartfelt devotion, also falls on its own petard when one reads the account of God casting the fallen angels into the fires of hell at the end of time in the Book of Revelations (Rev. 20:10). Clearly, God is fully capable of and willing to torment his creation for their rebellion at the end of time, so why doesn't that ultimate fate for rejecting him carry the same connotations now? Further, couldn't one make the case that destroying such an entity would be far more compassionate than eternally torturing it and, as such, more consistent with a loving creator?

Another problem is that even if we should allow for the possibility that God needed to create the angels for some reason and, further, that their ability to rebel was a necessary element of that creation, then how is it possible, if God is far more powerful than Satan (and Satan's army is vastly outnumbered in any case, as is generally believed and taught) for this demon army still to be fighting? If Satan's ill-fated rebellion has been going on since the creation of man, it seems God should have had plenty of time and, one would think, opportunity to finish the job. The fact that fighting is still raging, then, clearly implies that either God's army is utterly incompetent, or he is not as serious about stopping the devil as it is assumed. Since it is impossible to imagine an all-powerful God capable of fielding an incompetent army, however, this suggests the latter option, which is that God has no real interest in stopping Satan or his legion of followers. However, if God does not want to destroy this rebellion—remarkable in light of how destructive it has proven to be to his creation—that means God must want Satan and his demon army to exist, which further suggests that God intentionally created Satan for precisely this purpose (perhaps to test humanity's allegiance to him). If true, however, what does that say about God and his love?

Further, does this also not suggest that light and darkness can not only coexist in much the same way that matter and antimatter can exist within the same universe, but that they might even be necessary for the other to be realized? In effect, for evil to exist in a universe of love would entail a loving Creator permitting it to exist. Otherwise, God cannot be omnipotent. But this has profound implications, for if we imagine that nothing exists that God does not permit to exist, we have to assume that God fully *allows* and even *intended* for evil to be a part of the mix. This makes the current situation on this planet, then, essentially God's fault, for the evil that humanity performs could not occur apart from his will. In essence, for Satan and his demons to exist essentially makes God culpable for all the evil that has since resulted.

There are other objections as well, but this should be sufficient to demonstrate that the idea that there exists literal beings we call demons presents more theological and moral difficulties than it answers. Certainly, as far as the paranormal is concerned, it does little more than muddy the waters, for suggesting that God and Satan are effectively cocreators of the physical realm renders all notions of a kind and loving God—and, by extension, a good and loving supernatural realm—untenable. Either we live in a basically good and loving universe, of which God is the ultimate expression of that love, or life is a brutal and savage struggle between the forces of evil and those of an either inept and limited but essentially good God or a God that is in league with the devil, making him every bit as wicked as the very being he is supposed to be opposing.

All I can say is that if demons do, in fact, exist, it is evidence of a wholly incompetent Creator whose mismanagement of the universe has led to thousands of years of pain and misery and a hell brimming over with lost souls, a position I believe to be inconsistent with the belief in a God who is all-loving, all-powerful, and all-knowing. Either demons and Satan are real and God is a befuddled old man, or demons and Satan are a product of our own imagination and fears, and the universe is essentially benign.

Conclusion

For these reasons, as well as a host of other objections I have not touched upon here, I personally believe demons and Satan in general should remain in the realm of mythology and folklore where they belong, for I do not believe they are real spiritual entities. Many will argue with that conclusion, of course, and I am content to permit them their opinion, but I reject the idea on the grounds that the notion of demons simply is not morally defensible. While I am perfectly open to the idea that there are malevolent entities in existence—both human and nonhuman—I suspect them to be anomalous and rare beings that are trapped on the physical plane as a result of their own anger and confusion and that they are not the creation of either a benevolent God nor are they commanded by some twisted "super demon" (aka Satan). We discussed malevolent spirits in the last chapter, so it is not necessary to rehash the issue here; all I will add is that the phenomenon of demons can be solved without appealing to religious imagery or ancient mythology. Either they can be explained away as malevolent personalities that wander the periphery of our consciousness (and might be quite content with being thought of as "demons," even if there is no such thing), or they are a product of our own minds.

Or could they be a bit of both?

chapter ten

The Remarkable Story of Jack Maxwell

Jack Maxwell was about as down-to-earth a man as one is likely to meet. A retired Navy chief petty officer with a wife and two teenage kids, Jack Maxwell (not his real name) did not fit the evangelical born-again Christian mold, but this burly, powerfully built man with the handlebar mustache and dancing blue eyes seemed almost to burst with religious fervor.

Having only embraced Christianity myself a few weeks earlier, I had to admit I found him more than a little intimidating. I had seen born-again types before (and was technically even one myself), but never had I seen anyone so "into" his faith. He just didn't seem the type, at least not from my omniscient twenty-one-year-old perspective. Little did I realize it at the time, but Jack was to become my spiritual mentor during these early months of my newfound faith and would ultimately become the template off which I would gage my own spiritual progress. He was a type of spiritual barometer that would determine which of the beliefs I held to were "orthodox" and which were "heretical." Through his tutelage I learned more about Christianity in eight months than I did in the two decades of my life up to then, and my faith grew by leaps and bounds, largely because of his efforts. No doubt about it, Jack was easily one of the most influential people in my life, and I still find myself occasionally thinking fondly of him twenty-five years later.

The reason I bring Jack up was not just because of the impact he had on my life (though it was considerable), but because of what brought him to the point of acquiring such evangelical zeal in the first place. Jack, it seems, became such an ardent Christian because of the devil.

I know it sounds a little strange to imagine that Lucifer—aka Satan—could be responsible for a man's conversion to Christianity, but according to Jack that's exactly what happened. It seems that he hadn't always been an ardent Christian, he confided to me one night during one of our beloved "bull sessions." In fact, for the first forty years of his life he was a nominal Christian at best (to hear him tell it, nominal might have even been a considerable improvement over his self-declared debased lifestyle). So "nominal" was he, in fact, that he even managed to find himself in an adulterous affair with a young woman he had known for many years—an affair that came tantalizingly close to destroying his marriage.

Fortunately, much to Jack's credit, he just couldn't remain the scoundrel he imagined himself to be and, apparently recognizing the precarious state of his marriage and feeling a growing sense of guilt over his immoral ways, he decided to break it off with the young woman and make amends with his wife of twenty years. While this would normally seem to be the end of his troubles, that's when, in fact, they actually started, for it turned out that his spurned lover, unbeknownst to my friend, was much more than just another attractive woman. She was, in reality, a witch—and a witch with a very mean streak.

Of course, I had heard of people claiming to be witches before, but as far as I could tell such people do not seem either to possess magical powers nor do they generally appear particularly dangerous. This witch, however, was different. She was not some self-proclaimed witch who dressed head-to-toe in black, enjoyed dabbling in the occult, and carried the Book of Shadows around with her. Instead, she was—at least according to Jack—a real, full-fledged, Satan worshipping, black magic, card-carrying denizen of darkness type witch.[31] Further, not only was she intent on revenge, but she was in the process of trying to have old Jack possessed by demons as part of a greater plot to destroy him and his family.

That is when the story really got interesting. According to Jack, she apparently called a meeting of her coven sisters, and together they unleashed the hounds of hell against my befuddled friend, who suddenly found his home invaded by a host of entities intent on destroying him and his wife. Fortunately, Jack and his wife, Lynn, had recently become involved in a Pentecostal (or charismatic) church that believed in the protective powers of the Holy Spirit and, thus armed with the "whole armor of God,"[32] they were able to confront these invisible entities with a courage and strength borne of faith. After an evening of spiritual battle (during which their house was badly torn up), they successfully cast the entities out, and the immediate danger passed. He had to remain "prayed up" continually ever since, he told me, so that Satan was not afforded another opportunity to destroy him, thus explaining why he had to maintain such a high degree of spiritual vigor.

Remarkable story, I thought at the time, and to a kid whose ability to discern fact from fiction was somewhat suspect to begin with, a completely believable one. Certainly, Jack did not seem irrational nor did he appear prone toward storytelling (plus he had his wife and children to back up his fantastic claims) so I had little choice but to accept his story as fact, and for the next twenty years I believed it

---

31. Of course, most Wiccans would resent this description of themselves and reject the notion that they have anything to do with Satan or "black" magic. However, my purpose here is to demonstrate my friend's mind-set toward witches from the perspective of an evangelical Christian, which is necessary if we are to better understand how the circumstances he was to eventually find himself in could have come about. No offense is intended.

32. Ephesians 6:11 (New Testament).

without question. To this day I consider it the source from which much of my own previous fear of demons generated.

The years have a way of challenging and, when necessary, altering one's perspective, however, and today I no longer believe that Jack was attacked by demons. I don't believe such entities exist—at least not as they're portrayed in religious mythology—and as such, I do not believe that one can be possessed by a demon. On the other hand, I don't believe Jack was lying or fantasizing either. He truly believed he had been attacked by invisible malevolent forces, and I, for one, have no desire to challenge him on the point. Obviously, something happened to my friend those many years ago (and I've encountered a few similar stories since then as well), but what was it? Was it mass hallucination? Religion-driven hysteria? A psychotic episode? While it is tempting to write the entire incident off as evidence of the power of suggestion, I wonder if there could have been more at work here. I can't say with any degree of certainty exactly what it was, but I do have an idea. I suspect the source of Jack's troubles was all in his head—and, by that, I don't mean he imagined it. Instead, I believe he created it. Through the power of his own mind.

A Demon-Haunted World or the Power of the Mind?

I tell this story not in an attempt to belittle or repudiate the sincerely held religious beliefs of a man whom I respect and admire very much, but in an effort to demonstrate the remarkable powers of the mind and the way superstition may allow malevolent spirits to enter into our lives. If there are no such things as demons, as I have suggested, then it is possible that accounts of especially malicious entities that have been recorded over the centuries may be more a product of our minds than we might imagine. I don't mean that they are imaginary or mere hallucinations, but instead that they are things we give form to via the energy of our own thoughts. In essence, I propose that in many cases, malevolent entities may be a manifestation brought about by our own subconscious beliefs, presumptions, and fears that work together to manifest what we call demons.

That the mind is capable of remarkable things is indisputable. Hypnotized subjects being told that a liquid is sour when it is in fact quite sweet have been observed to pucker their lips and make faces when tasting it, while cases of individuals having allergic reactions to certain foods they believed they had ingested—but in reality had not—have also been recorded. Suggestion has always been a tried-and-true method of inducing certain physical responses in people, which anyone who has ever witnessed a "miracle healing crusade" can attest to: headaches and backaches instantly vanish, arthritis pain remarkably subsides, feeling in a numb limb is miraculously restored. Additionally, virulent cancers have been seen to go into spontaneous remission in patients who have prayed for a healing, while studies have repeatedly shown that the severity and frequency of illnesses are often significantly reduced among people who maintain a positive attitude. Evidence that the human body shows a remarkable ability to correspond to the emotional state of the mind? Perhaps, although a positive attitude is not always successful in restoring and retaining good health. Sometimes optimistic people get sick and die while pessimists somehow go on and on, but if the human body responds to the emotional state of the mind even ten percent of the time, that is still significant.

An even more spectacular demonstration of the power of the mind to affect one's physiology can be seen in the phenomenon of the "hex" or "death curse." Anthropologists who have studied primitive cultures in detail have documented a surprising number of cases of otherwise perfectly healthy villagers growing sick and dying within days of being told the tribal witch doctor had put a curse on them. Conversely, outsiders who interacted with these tribes and ran afoul of the village witch doctor themselves suffered no similar effects when told they had the same curse put on them.[33] So why did they not die when their study subjects did? Apparently, it was simply because they did not believe in curses whereas their unfortunate hosts did, demonstrating, then, that belief can not only produce measurable physiological changes in a person, but in the hands of the devoutly superstitious, can even apparently kill.

The stigmata—the inexplicable ability demonstrated by a handful of very devout religious figures throughout history to manifest the marks of Jesus' crucifixion on their hands and feet—is an even more remarkable example of how strongly held beliefs can manifest themselves physiologically. Medical authorities who have had the opportunity to examine this extraordinary phenomenon in those rare individuals who exhibit this ability consistently eliminate self-mutilation as an explanation, thus leaving science at a loss to explain how bleeding, nail-like wounds can spontaneously appear on otherwise healthy tissue and remain impervious to the body's natural healing and clotting abilities for days or even weeks at a time.[34] What's even more curious about this phenomenon, however—and most telling—is that throughout history, stigmatics have traditionally borne these marks on the palms of the hand, precisely as depicted in religious imagery of the era. Recently, however, scholars have come to the conclusion that nails would need to have been driven through the crucifixion victim's wrist in order to sustain their body weight on the cross, and so almost overnight stigmatics began showing an issuance of blood coming from the "correct" spot on the wrist, which is the best evidence yet that it is the mind and not something supernatural that is behind these marks.

---

33. See the work of anthropologist Joan Halifax-Grof ("Hex Death" in *Parapsychology and Anthropology: Proceedings of an International Conference*. New York: Parapsychology Foundation, 1974), as well as other works.

34. One explanation that has been suggested to explain this well-documented phenomenon is that certain blood vessels in the appropriate spots on the body may actually be made to swell and burst, creating an issuance of blood that perfectly mimics the marks of the Crucifixion. For a detailed discussion of this phenomenon and the power of hypnotically induced suggestion to effect physiological changes in the body, refer to chapter 2, "Bodily Changes Corresponding to Mental Images in the Person Affected," in *Reincarnation and Biology, Vol. 1: Birthmarks*, by Dr. Ian Stevenson (Praegor Publishers, 1997).

As such, if the power of belief has the ability to manufacture physical manifestations of the crucifixion on a saint's body and even lead to the deaths of people in certain primitive cultures, then what does this say about belief in general?

That it is powerful.

Powerful enough to heal and, perhaps, even powerful enough to kill in some cases, despite science's insistence that such is purely coincidental nonsense.

But what does this have to do with demons? Everything, it seems, for if that same power of suggestion is directed in the proper way, might it not be capable of manifesting precisely the object the believer is most afraid of—in this case, a demonic entity? Is such an idea not at least worth considering?

Actually, the idea that one's state of mind might be capable of conjuring up a "demon" should be no more remarkable than is the idea that a cynic's pessimistic outlook might be capable of inadvertently creating the conditions in their body that makes them ripe for cancerous cell growth. Yet what is important to recognize is that just as the pessimist's cancer is empirically real, so too may be the hysterical person's "demon" as well. Even if one's state of mind may not create the realities the body experiences, it could potentially create the conditions conducive for certain realities to manifest themselves. All it may take is belief.

The Power of Fear

As such, what I believe my friend Jack experienced was not an attack from a legion of demons, but the manifestation of negative energies trying to feed off his own fear. In effect, both Jack and his "demons" were feeding off each other; his fear fueling their manifestations and their manifestations fueling his belief in their existence. It wasn't until he grew unafraid of them, I believe, that they finally lost their power and faded, while at the same time confirming his suspicions that demons were real (and, with it, the idea that witches really could call up demons and send them to do their bidding). Labeling such energies "demons" then was simply his way of making sense of the encounter, as well as further fueling his almost obsessive religiosity.

But how did these entities manifest in the first place? Could the self-proclaimed witch really have sent them, or did he create them from his own mind? Could his guilt and fear over his adulterous affair—along with his inherent belief in demons and witchcraft—have created the proper conditions that a malevolent spirit required to manifest itself? In essence, might not Jack's own superstitions have triggered the paranormal activity in the same way that nervous energy from a high-strung adolescent might be utilized by a mischievous entity to move objects across a room in typical poltergeist fashion? Certainly, if a mischievous ghost (or a group of them) were looking for the ideal conditions under which to manifest, my friend Jack would have been the perfect vehicle for them. In fact, I can't imagine how such entities could have passed up such an opportunity, especially when it was handed to them on a silver platter.

I'll probably never know if Jack was actually victimized by such entities or if he imagined the whole series of events himself, and I suspect he remains to this day unshakable in his belief that he was attacked by demons at the behest of an ex-lover's bidding. Whether Jack's answer to what happened to him is naïvely simplistic or unnecessarily complex is unimportant; it does, however, demonstrate that there are more things in heaven and earth than we have dreamed of in our philosophies, and among them are the powers of the mind and the ability of negative entities to make themselves known in our world—if we let them in.

Conclusion

Undoubtedly this argument will do little to dissuade the true believer that demons are, at worst, simply another name for malevolent ghosts, nor is it likely to alter the skeptic's beliefs that demons are nothing more than the power of suggestion and a fervent imagination working in tandem, but then that is not the purpose of this book. I only wish to ask the questions and offer one alternative among many that may be possible. My point being that if ghosts do exist and are capable of manifesting themselves within our physical realm, we must accept the possibility and, indeed, the likelihood that they may be far more interactive than we have previously imagined, and, as such, could well be the explanation for much of what passes for "demonic activity." In the end, then, demons may be nothing more than primitive man's attempt to understand and define these energies by using the only models—the belief in various gods and the power of nature—available to them.

Finally, if the power of belief is capable of manifesting a room full of "demons"—as may have been the case with my friend Jack—could it also be the explanation for the most controversial aspect of the supernatural, demonic possession? Before completing our examination of the dark side of the supernatural, it is necessary that we briefly pause to consider this issue as well, for in doing so we may find not only a new and better understanding of how the supernatural realm works, but come to appreciate the power of the mind in all its many manifestations, of which the belief that one is possessed by a demon may be the most remarkable.

chapter eleven

A Look at Demonic Possession

W hen I was a boy, the movie *The Exorcist* was a big hit with the movie-going public. The story of a twelve-year-old girl unsuccessfully fighting off the efforts of a demon to possess her is considered to this day to be one of the great horror flicks of all time.

What was most remarkable about the movie, however, was not its chilling special effects or even the story itself, but the fact that within weeks of its release, scores of people around the country began reporting that they—or someone they knew—were similarly possessed by a demon (much to the consternation of the mental health community), and almost overnight exorcism and possession became hot topics. Even today, forty years later, the possibility of being possessed remains a strongly maintained belief in some quarters, giving birth to a library of books and movies on the subject and even producing entire ministries devoted exclusively to healing people unfortunate enough to be so afflicted.

So what are we to make of this? Is it all so much superstitious nonsense, reinforced by Hollywood and encouraged by religious zealots of all stripes, or is there something to it? It seems disingenuous to simply dismiss the possibility out of hand based purely upon the opinion of science that there is no such thing as demons and, as such, possession. After all, stories of possession have been a part of our cultural beliefs as long as there has been organized religion (and long before Hollywood got involved). Further, there are several fairly well-documented cases of alleged demonic possession on record that need to be considered as well, so the subject of whether a person truly can be possessed is an important one that needs to be addressed if we are to make this as complete a study on the subject of spiritual entities as intended.

Possession

No doubt the first possibility one normally entertains when dealing with a well-documented case of demon possession is that it is either a case of severe psychosis or, perhaps, evidence of a multiple personality disorder (MPD), either of which could account for many of the symptoms generally attributed to possession. This, of course, would be the simplest approach and, as such, the one generally favored by most skeptics. However, this does not necessarily make it the best explanation, especially in light of the fact that it fails to take into account that mental health care facilitators are usually quite adept at identifying such disorders, making it highly unlikely that someone suffering from either psychosis or MPD could be easily misdiagnosed as being demonically possessed (especially by a health professional who does not believe in the existence of demons in the first place). Additionally, many religious practitioners[35] and those who deal with supposed cases of possession on a regular basis are normally equally careful about ensuring that they are not dealing with a person suffering from mental illness before taking the step of declaring an individual possessed. The Catholic church, for example, goes to great lengths to find medical or psychological explanations for every case of alleged possession it encounters, making it further unlikely that a person suffering from a classic psychological disorder would be labeled as possessed, at least in modern times.[36] Clearly, even people who believe in demons recognize that there is more to a

---

35. Unfortunately, there are still many amateur exorcists and religious novices out there who are quick to presume possession, making it extremely important that the careful researcher approaches the subject with a healthy dose of skepticism.

36. Before the advent of modern psychology, however, no doubt many mentally disturbed individuals were proclaimed to be possessed, a fact that even the Catholic church has publicly acknowledged over the years, which probably accounts for the more careful and reasoned methodology it employs today.

possession than mere delusional ramblings and competing personalities masquerading as otherworldly entities.

However, sometimes cases come along that do not fit either the classic psychosis or MPD models and so do suggest that some kind of external entity might be at work. But what could it be? Is a disembodied personality really capable of somehow attaching itself to the human psyche in a way that the victim/host loses all capacity to resist? In other words, could someone really be "possessed" against their will (with or without all the theatrics of a Hollywood production), or is there some other, more prosaic, answer? While there are several possible explanations, I believe we might find the answer by looking at a well-witnessed incident of supposed possession culled from the distant past and recorded in the Bible—the one book, one would think, that should know whereof it speaks when it comes to such things as demonic possession. Let's see what this ancient book can tell us, if anything, about what demonic possession may genuinely be.

The Gerasenes Case: A Demon Parasite or a Sick Mind?

While the Bible contains several accounts of apparent demons interacting with the physical world, one story in particular stands out. The eighth chapter of the Gospel of Luke (verses 26–38) records the remarkable story of a supposedly demon-possessed man that Jesus and his disciples encountered near a small village named Gerasenes on the shores of the Sea of Galilee. Met on the beach as they landed by a naked man (a parallel account in Matthew lists two men) who screamed and shouted at them, Jesus calmly engaged the obviously crazed man in conversation and learned that he was possessed by a number of demons. Identifying themselves collectively as "legion" and begging Jesus not to "send them away" (apparently, they were quite afraid that Jesus would send them somewhere they did not want to be, though it is not stated where this someplace was), in something of a compromise, Jesus permitted the demons to enter into a nearby herd of pigs, which promptly stampeded and flung themselves into the lake and drowned, after which the man almost immediately came to his right mind and calmed down. Even more remarkable, and potentially telling, the man then asked if he might not join Jesus and become one of his disciples, a request that Jesus gently declined.

This is an interesting story, unusually rich in detail, that has a certain air of authenticity about it. Even though Matthew's account differs from that told in Luke's gospel in terms of the number of individuals Jesus encountered and a few other minor details, it appears to have been a real event that actually occurred and, further, one that was witnessed by a large number of people (most importantly, among them being nonbelievers and gentiles), which would seem to preclude it from being purely fictional or completely hearsay and, as such, demands that we deal with it seriously.

So what do we make of it, and, more importantly, what does it have to tell us about the spiritual realm, if anything?

It has much to say if one takes the time to "read between the lines" and ask a few simple questions.

For example, what first strikes me about the story is how well this man exhibited all the classic signs of psychosis: the self-inflicted wounds, the tendency to chase people, reports of great strength (though not observed in the Gospel account). The man was clearly delusional and obviously in agony (not just physically, but psychologically as well). We cannot know all that was going on—for example, we know nothing of his personal history or whether this "possession" came on him suddenly or gradually over a period of time—but it was apparent he was considered possessed by the people living nearby as evidenced by their statements and attempts to chain him.

The real question is not whether others thought him possessed, however, but whether *he* considered himself possessed. This is important, for it answers several questions. First, and most obviously, it answers why a supposedly malevolent parasitic spirit would have the man run to the one place it would put itself in greatest danger: into the very presence of Jesus himself.

I may not know much about demonic logic, but if I were taking up residence in someone's body and didn't want to be cast out, I should think that running to Jesus would be the last thing I would do. The story would make more sense if Jesus and the disciples had chased the man down or had him brought before them in chains by villagers anxious to relieve the man of his suffering; the fact that the demoniac took the initiative to approach Jesus is significant. Does it not beg the question of why it would do so if not because it *wanted* to be cast out?

As such, is it possible the man was convinced he was possessed and, like anyone with a debilitating disease, went to Jesus for healing? Considering that in those days psychological disorders were unknown, making any mental health problem—from mild neurosis to full-blown psychosis—naturally assumed to be a product of demonic affliction, it makes perfect sense that the man would interpret his own psychotic episodes as evidence of possession and act accordingly. But even then, why go to Jesus for healing? Even if he had convinced himself he was possessed, what rationale would he have for pursuing an exorcism? In essence, why not just maintain the delusion and leave it at that?

Apparently a part of the man knew he was sick and wanted to be healed. Many mental health professionals are convinced that the human psyche maintains a built-in self-correcting mechanism that endeavors to restore mental health when it is out of balance (just as the body attempts to restore good health when it is out of whack). That being the case then, could the Gerasenes "demoniac" have simply been a man with a serious psychological disorder—naturally interpreted as demonic possession at the time—who found the courage and the opportunity to take the steps required to restore his own mental health (albeit in a religious context)? Undoubtedly he had heard of this itinerant rabbi with miraculous powers and had come to believe he really was, if not a god, at least a great prophet of God, and so he sought him out when he learned of his arrival. Such would make perfect sense and be in keeping with what modern psychology has observed in people suffering from various mental disorders who consciously seek out help rather than being forced into treatment.

Further, at least in this case, it seemed his tactic, fueled by his fervent beliefs and superstitions, worked. No eight-hour marathon exorcism here, but just a few simple words and the man was "back in his right mind" and begging to be included as one of Jesus' disciples. Notice the remarkable transition from demoniac to disciple in just a few minutes; there is not another example of such a rapid conversion recorded in the gospels. In fact, this is the only man recorded in scripture who specifically requested to be a disciple—the others being essentially draftees! Even more significant, this is the one man Jesus did not allow to follow him, instead telling him to return to his home and tell others what had happened. Did Jesus understand something about the man and the situation at hand that no one else on hand seemed to recognize?

The Power of Belief

According to many reputable sources, no one who has ever been "possessed" by a demon did not believe in demons beforehand. Further, it is reported that victims of possession often come from deeply religious backgrounds and are many times considered almost "saintly" in their devotion to God both before and after their exorcism. Well-known author and psychologist Dr. M. Scott Peck records in his excellent book *People of the Lie*[37] that this was true of the three cases of possession he reputedly personally witnessed; each victim displayed an extraordinary devotion to God at some point earlier in their life and returned to it again after their exorcism. Though Dr. Peck decided these were legitimate examples of true demonic possession, I wonder if he didn't miss a clue here. Is it possible that extreme religious faith, combined with a genuine psychological disorder, might not manifest itself as a possession in keeping with the religious beliefs of one's cul-

---

37. Dr. M. Scott Peck, *People of the Lie* (Simon & Schuster, 1983).

ture and time? (It's further telling to note that as far as anyone can tell, no atheist has ever been possessed by a demon. Coincidence or something more?)

I believe the imagination, when combined with fervent belief, might be quite capable, in certain hypersensitive individuals, of producing the standard "marks" of demonic possession: inhuman, blasphemous speech, grisly facial expressions, even great adrenaline-induced strength. Such an idea is not without precedence: in the rare mental disorder known as lycanthropy, the patient becomes convinced he is a wolf and will demonstrate wolf-like characteristics such as running on all fours, snarling and biting, and howling at the moon. Are we to assume such would have been impossible in the case of the Gerasanes demoniac? Was Jesus faced with, then, not a foreign entity, but merely a fantasy-prone and deeply superstitious mind masquerading as a case of demon possession?

True, the "entity" is recorded as having spoken to Jesus, even identifying itself by name, but what sort of proof is that? Could that not simply have been just another manifestation of the patient's own imagination? The "entity" did not speak in some unknown language, nor did it express any unique supernatural knowledge or abilities that might suggest something external was behind the man's problems. Could it have been nothing more than his own imagination speaking, saying what he *imagined* a demon might say?

But what of the swine that stampeded to their death the moment the "demons" were cast out of the man? How do we explain this spectacular and unexpected reaction from nonsentient creatures who lacked the capacity to either believe or disbelieve in demons? Surely that demonstrated external forces were at work, did it not?

Again, it may have been unfortunately necessary for the man's healing. He had asked that the demons not be "sent away" (to where, we know not) but instead be sent into the herd of nearby pigs. I believe Jesus reluctantly relented for the sake of the man's healing by supernaturally manifesting a panic reflex in at least some of the herd. Spook a few swine and the rest might also be similarly panicked (much like a stampede among cattle), giving the appearance of a demonic-possessed herd of swine in full flight. Their subsequent drowning, in fact, might well have been unintentional: driven by momentum and gravity, they may have simply inadvertently flung themselves into the too-close water, which, while unfortunate and unintentional, would have had the effect of further dramatizing the event.[38] (For that matter, could the observing crowd have spooked the herd at a most inopportune moment? Animals are known to respond to strong human emotions, of which fear is among the most powerful. Could the pigs—one of the more intelligent of mammals—have picked up on the negative energy the crowd was sending out and responded to it by taking flight? It is an intriguing possibility.)

In any case, it worked. Now convinced he was free of the demons, his underlying psychosis at last had a chance to heal. Obviously a pious man, he begged to go with Jesus, only to be told no. I believe Jesus refused because he saw a fervency that bordered on the fanatical, which was not what he needed from the disciples. He would have been only trouble if he had come with them, especially around Jesus—the apparent object of his newfound adoration. Such an unstable psyche, even if healed of its previous chemical imbalances, might still be too delicate to survive the tribulations of Calvary, and so Jesus sent him away for his own good.

But what of the imaginary demons, then? If Jesus knew the man was suffering from psychosis and not demonic possession, why not come right out and tell the crowds? Is he not being deceptive if he simply plays along with the idea of possession, even if it was ultimately for the greater good?

Not necessarily. First, how does Jesus explain to his unsophisticated and illiterate listeners—simple farmers, shepherds, and fisherman—about the reality of chemical imbalances in the brain? Clearly, in such a primitive world, his audience could not begin to understand, and so

---

38. Unfortunately, this suggests culpability on the part of Jesus, who may have only instilled fear into them to effect the healing without foreseeing their flight to the water. They did, after all, constitute somebody's livelihood, making it unlikely Jesus would have had them intentionally drown themselves.

he did the only thing he could do: play along. On the other hand, perhaps in being a product of that world himself, Jesus really believed he was dealing with demons and in so doing inadvertently healed the man of his condition in the process of dealing with them. In either case, whether there was or was not a genuine demon involved, there was genuine healing, both emotionally and spiritually, and that is what Jesus' ministry was all about.

Of course, this is just one story of several the Bible records and only one of potentially dozens or more that have been documented throughout the centuries, so it is hardly conclusive. However, there seems to be an underlying pattern to possession stories that this particular story illustrates so well: an (assumedly) previously held, culturally enhanced belief in demons, symptoms of psychosis (the inability to determine fantasy from reality), an unusual need to attract attention to oneself, especially in public places (presumably so the "demon" can be noticed, confronted, and finally "cast out"), and a high degree of piousness or renewed sense of religiosity in the aftermath of the successful exorcism. Take any of the four elements out of the mix, and it seems that demons do not manifest very well.

Malevolent Parasites and Exorcisms

While this suggests a purely psychological cause behind possession, the thought that there could be malevolent parasites that might attach themselves to an individual cannot be entirely dismissed. In chapter eight we discussed how these entities might operate and what effect they could have on a human host, so the fact that even if demons themselves may be a figment of our imagination or some residual superstition from a long-ago era, that does not preclude the possibility that there may be dangerous entities out there we need to be cautious of. I doubt they could take over an individual to the point that one loses all control over themselves, but it is entirely possible they could so influence a person—or reinforce the negative energy already inherent in them—as to impel them to commit heinous crimes of remarkable brutality. As such, reports of "demons" and "possession" should not be taken lightly, for they could be harbingers of real danger and, on occasion, even evidence of something genuinely supernatural taking place.

Of course, if true, this brings up the possibility of whether such a ritual as exorcism might be necessary to aid in a "possessed" patient's recovery. After all, if one either truly believes one is possessed or is genuinely afflicted with a persistent or even malicious spiritual parasite, it would seem the rites of exorcism might well prove beneficial to the sufferer. In fact, some who operate exorcism ministries insist it is the only way to free one of these parasites, and they go about casting out demons with an often remarkable zeal and determination.

In the Bible story we just recounted, it seemed that just such a "ritual" (if it could be called that) did the trick. All that was necessary for the man to be healed was Jesus simply ordering the offending spirits to depart, and all was well. Even if the offending spirits in this case were purely a figment of the man's imagination, he seemed to "need" to be exorcised of them; in fact, it would be difficult to see how the man could have been convinced that the demons were gone any other way. As such, an "exorcism" might well have beneficial effects for those who are convinced they are truly possessed, particularly as it feeds into their already deeply held beliefs and superstitions. In that way, then, an exorcism would have a type of placebo effect in convincing especially suggestible persons that the demons had left and, in so doing, bring them into their right mind.

There is a problem, however. It has been frequently noted that people who have had demons apparently "cast out" have been frequently observed to have them return later, so this may not be the permanent cure it portends to be. Obviously, a deeply delusional person is probably not going to be permanently convinced they are free of demons unless the underlying psychosis is also dealt with; in effect, the cure will last only as long as the victim allows it to, in precisely the same way that a placebo will eliminate symptoms only as long as the sufferer believes it will. Once the experience fades (as it is bound to do after a few days), the underlying fantasy may return in full force and, in fact, may even be strengthened by having undergone an exorcism ritual, which may have had the unintended consequences of reinforcing the original delusion even further.

On the other hand, if the problem is not psychosomatic but the result of genuine external spiritual entities, it is not clear how an exorcism would be useful. Unless we assume the very act of exorcism itself contains some "magical" ability to force an unwanted entity to flee, we can presume it will be useful only to the degree the entity permits it to be. In effect, if the malicious spirit *believes* the exorcism has the ability to make it leave (perhaps because it held similar religious convictions while in the flesh), it may well move on, whereas an entity that held to no such beliefs—or is even contemptuous of them—may well play along with the charade until either the exorcist gives up or the entity tires of the game and moves on to another, less problematic host. Of course, it is also possible that such a ritual could even have the unanticipated effect of forcing the entity further "underground"—that is, deeper into the host's psyche—until it appears to be gone, but is in fact still in residence, though now in a less obvious fashion. In effect, a particularly malignant entity might learn to play dead and then manifest itself within its victim's psyche in far more subtle and less discernible— but no less intrusive or even destructive—ways in the future, making it even more potentially troublesome.

In the end, however, it may be the victim themselves that finally determines whether an entity stays or goes, and this will be true whether the individual is suffering from either the delusion of demonic infestation or is genuinely being tormented by external personalities. In other words, once the host no longer needs the delusion or is unwilling to provide the prerequisite energy a malevolent entity requires to manifest itself, the "demon" may have no choice but to leave, permitting the symptoms to eventually subside or cease altogether. Perhaps that's the reason why possessions often appear to be so enduring and demons so difficult to exorcise; it's because the person becomes convinced they "need" the entity in some way, making its ability to manifest even more pronounced. As I said earlier, the mind truly is responsible for one's spiritual state, whether that state be good or bad.

As far as whether individuals should take on the role of "casting out" demons themselves, this is something that is probably better left to the experts. If one is dealing with a delusional personality, such efforts might not only be counterproductive but even potentially dangerous. One may be dealing with an unstable personality who would be better served by a mental health professional than by a rank amateur, so I would be especially cautious about attempting any home-grown exorcism rites with an individual who is convinced they are possessed. In the end it could do more harm than good.

Further, if one really is dealing with malevolent entities, such entities may likely resent being accused of being a demon or told to leave. In fact, the evidence suggests that an exorcism is likely to provoke them to even more violence, so one is probably better off not to even address such a being. Additionally, it is possible that since we know nothing of the mental states of these entities themselves, they might well be convinced they *are* demons and so could take on some decidedly "demonic" characteristics (such as writhing and howling and cursing, for example; things a "demon" might be expected to do). This might explain why some supposedly possessed people—speaking in some otherworldly voice—proclaim themselves to be Satan or admit to being a demon; the entities that are influencing them either really believe they are demons or they have a decidedly sick sense of humor and are merely playing along.[39] In either case, they are undoubtedly unstable personalities and, as such, are best left alone.

Finally, it is possible that there are genuinely horrific extra-celestials or nonhuman personalities out there who may truly be "demonic" in nature and, as such, need to be taken into account (in fact, such creatures may be the source behind much demonic mythology, the religious context into which they eventually emerged being a later con-

---

39. In some cases, if the "possession" is entirely psychosomatic and there is no evidence of otherworldly entities, the victims themselves may inadvertently "create" demons out of their imagination and speak for them. Such a case would again demonstrate the power of superstition to manifest otherworldly manifestations where none exists.

fabulation designed to explain how such beings came into existence in an essentially benevolent universe). Such beings, assuming they exist, really could be dangerous and should be given a wide berth if one suspects one is dealing with such a creature. However, I suspect, as I stated earlier, that such entities would have trouble operating freely in a truly benign universe and might well be opposed by more benevolent spiritual beings whose role it is to limit their impact upon the physical realm. That could be why, if such beings exist at all, they may need to be invited or attracted into our world and are prevented from doing so unless they are given that invitation.

Of course, all of this is highly speculative. There may, in fact, be no such thing as a malevolent extra-celestials at all, much in the same way that there may not be such things as demons in the realm of the absolute. However, I still find it likely that there are angry, hateful, spiteful people in the spiritual realm just as there are in the physical realm, and that should be enough to keep us wary. The universe is a very big and still largely unexplored place, so we would be wise to proceed with caution where things like negative energies are concerned, both in this world and in the next.

Conclusion

While it seems unlikely the average person will ever encounter a genuinely possessed person or experience being in the presence of a truly malevolent entity, the fact that such things may exist must be taken into account. Additionally, we must also be willing to recognize the profound power of the human mind to create out of its vast storehouse of experiences and beliefs the very manifestations of those things it fears the most. Science is only beginning to unravel the intricacies of the human mind, much less to consider the vast mysteries of the universe around us, so we should not be too quick to either believe everything we see and hear, nor too hasty in dismissing everything as our imagination playing tricks on us. Beliefs do play a role in the nature of reality, as do genuine external energies that may be a small part of a much larger universal consciousness, so we would be wise to take both into account before rendering a verdict in regard to things like demons and possession. Religion's attempts to quantify and define these things are mere efforts at understanding a larger whole, and while it may have some things to say to the human condition and the nature of belief itself, it cannot answer the whole question. To assume that it can is to limit the scope of our investigation and overlook the more important lessons the universe has to show us, which in the end could prove counterproductive to the entire process of enlightenment and spiritual growth.

part four

Communicating with the Spirit Realm

Now that we have come to appreciate the mysterious nature of the supernatural realm and are becoming increasingly aware of the magnitude of life that may exist all around us, we can begin to discard the old models for understanding the paranormal and move into a more mature understanding of the issue. And a part of that new understanding is asking ourselves what's next. If ghosts are real, where do we go from here?

The most obvious answer, especially in that human beings are, by our very nature, naturally curious about what awaits us after death, is that we would want to find a way to tap into that realm for the answers. In essence, the next logical step is to ask ourselves whether we might not be able to communicate with these disembodied personalities and, if so, how we might go about doing so.

So just how does one communicate with what is little more than an immaterial cloud of human consciousness? It seems impossible, and yet the desire to do so, at least for some people, is overwhelming, especially when that cloud of disembodied energy may be a beloved family member or a close friend. But how might we go about it and, further, is such communication even possible? Can we interact with ghosts in meaningful ways, or are we always fated to be separated by a veil of inaccessibility due to our very different natures or realms of existence? Further, aren't we potentially asking for trouble if we start dabbling in this area and perhaps even opening the doors to all sorts of paranormal mischief?

While such is a valid concern (and a point we will examine in some detail in a moment) I suspect we may lose an important opportunity for growth if we refuse to consider the possibility. While there are those negative aspects of the supernatural realm to be aware of, I am convinced there are also those elements that are benevolent and helpful, and that we should be able to interact with those beings if we approach them with love, compassion, and openness. Of course, the skeptics will declare all such efforts fruitless and the religionists will call them dangerous, but if a spiritual realm exists at all and it is inhabited by legions of enlightened and wise individuals willing and able to interact with us, we would be foolish not to try to and reach out to them (or, at the very least, make ourselves open to them).

As such, in this section we will explore some ideas about how interaction between the physical and spiritual realms might be possible and what benefits that might hold for us. Additionally, we will also examine the controversial issue of spirit guides, which should provide us with an ever greater vista of possibilities to consider as we explore the world of the supernatural.

chapter twelve

Communicating with the Dead

When most people consider the issue of spirit communication, the first image that usually comes to mind is that of a medium speaking in otherworldly voices while holding hands with a circle of strangers in a darkened room. In other words, most people probably think of the traditional seance—an image Hollywood and, to a great extent, the paranormal community itself—has done much to encourage. Considering the prodigious amount of fraud such activity has been associated with over the years, however, makes it difficult to take this form of communication seriously. Images of shoddy, staged seances and cunning charlatans posing as mediums have been such a major element of the paranormal over the years that the practice is rarely taken seriously today by any but the most fervent believers, thereby bringing the entire possibility of spirit communication into question. But is that truly the case? Is communicating with the dead out of the question, or are there means available both to us and to the departed that might make such communication possible?

The answer is yes to the latter question. In fact, the average person may be surprised to learn that communicating with the dead may be easier than one might think and, further, that it requires no special training, equipment, or inherent paranormal powers to do so. All it takes is an openness to such communication being a possibility, some patience and perseverance, and the rest will take care of itself.

ADCs: The World of Spirit Speak

Stories of ghosts speaking to people—known as after death communication (ADCs)—while uncommon, are not unknown, as are stories of ghosts directly responding to the verbal statements of witnesses. Even remarkably interactive conversations with disembodied entities have been recorded, with conversations lasting several minutes and even longer being reported. Further, most people who have reported an interactive conversation with a ghost are often startled by the clarity and obviously natural quality such encounters frequently demonstrate, which would seem to suggest that at least some ghosts do seem to be able to communicate quite clearly if they wish to. But how do they accomplish this?

While there may be several possibilities to consider, the one theory that is growing increasingly popular (and that we looked at briefly in chapter four) is that ghosts communicate telepathically. The hearer only imagines the ghost is talking to them (it may even be mouthing words) but the witness is actually "hearing" the entity all within his or her head. In effect, we misidentify the source of the words as being external—that is, picked up by our natural auditory senses—whereas in fact it is internal and being perceived within the brain itself. However, while this idea may account for a percentage of ghostly conversations, it fails to explain those instances when ghosts have been reportedly heard by more than one person simultaneously or have had their "voices" recorded on audiotape, thus forcing us to conclude that at least some spirit communication is a genuine manifestation of physical energy of some kind. How it might be possible for a nonphysical energy to do this remains uncertain, of course, but then so is the process by which it might visibly manifest itself. Both processes, however, in being simply a matter of manipulating energy in various fashions, should be equally doable. In effect, if a ghost can manifest itself to us at all, it should be able to talk as well. It seems a package deal.

That being said, however, the ability to initiate a two-way audible communication with a spirit has proven to be extremely difficult to achieve and even more difficult to sustain, suggesting that the amount of energy required to carry on a conversation may be beyond the abilities of most spiritual entities. Yet it remains a fascinating possibility that promises extraordinary results were such communication capable of being achieved on a consistent basis and, most importantly of all, recorded in front of reliable witnesses. Before examining some possible theories as to how a ghost might be able to accomplish this, it may be beneficial to more closely examine the entire range of spirit communication and the myriad of ways ghosts may have of communicating with the living.

Spirit Telepathy: Speaking Through Mediums and Psychics

Despite the objections noted above, it still remains likely that the majority of ghostly communication is largely telepathic in nature. As such, if we are to expand our horizons in regard to the paranormal in general, we must be open to the idea that there could be those rare individuals who are capable of telepathically communicating with conscious energy on a consistent basis. We refer to such individuals by a number of different names, with medium being the most common, though psychic,[40] channeler, necromancer, or sensitive are also used. Whatever nomenclature they choose to go by, however, it is these people who theoretically make communication with the dead not only more readily possible, but potentially provable.

Unfortunately, years of fraud and self-deception have given the medium trade a bad name, but the idea that there could be people who can genuinely communicate with the dead should not be automatically dismissed. While extreme caution is necessary and a healthy dose of skepticism is essential when considering such claims, it is not unreasonable to imagine that if there is such a thing as a ghost, it is

---

40. A psychic is a broad term and can mean anyone with heightened extrasensory powers, of which the ability to communicate with the dead is only one. Therefore, not all psychics are capable of paranormal communication.

equally reasonable to imagine that there are those who are capable of interacting with it. But, if so, how does this communication work?

There appear to be several methods by which spiritual energies are able to communicate through these people. While most such communication appears to be conversational in nature (that is, an entity simply talking as it would were they still alive), there are those individuals who perceive this communication metaphorically. For example, the famous television psychic John Edward rarely claims that entities have spoken to him in clear phrases, but only that they send him images or symbols in his mind's eye that he then tries to decode or interpret. Sometimes he gets a name or a letter, but usually he sees places or symbols that his audience then attempts to interpret.[41] Additionally, unlike most mediums, he is not required to go to a particular physical location to contact an entity, but seems capable of communicating with it wherever he is. In effect, the spiritual entities come to him, which makes Edward—and the handful of noted mediums like him— unique in that respect.

Most mediums, however, must go to the physical location where an alleged haunting is taking place in order to perceive these entities (suggesting a particular spatial element inherent to ghostly manifestation). Additionally, unlike Edward's metaphorical communication, most mediums report their conversations with the dead to be quite natural and even chatty in nature. Many, in fact, appear to carry on rather complex conversations with spiritual entities (although, unfortunately, little of it appears to be rich in historical or verifiable details). In being able to obtain converse in such a relatively effortless method would seem to imply that telepathy may be the preferred method of spiritual communication, possibly due to its low energy requirements and enhanced clarity. In fact, it might be surmised that physically

---

41. While frequently dismissed as a master practitioner of the ancient art of "cold reading" (the practice of making random and generalized statements in the hopes that something will resonate with listeners and then reading their reactions to other similarly vague statements in an effort to convince them that they are in genuine communication with the spirit of a deceased loved one) many of Edward's statements are frequently specific enough to make the objective observer wonder.

manifested sound may be a "lesser" and certainly more difficult means of speaking, explaining its comparative rarity as a means of ghostly communication.

So is a medium a good means of communicating with the dead? It all depends upon the integrity of the medium and what sort of information one is hoping to acquire from an entity. While sometimes extremely interesting and even useful information is obtained, generally one is only going to get a few useful tidbits and probably no real follow-up, making it not a particularly useful means of proving the existence of ghosts. Legitimate mediums may be helpful in determining if and why a residence is haunted, but they are not particularly useful in developing a long-term relationship with an entity that could prove scientifically valid. Only if a medium were willing to work with an entity for a lengthy period of time would this method of communicating be worthwhile, and then only as long as medium and entity were willing to cooperate with each other.

Such a thing is not entirely unheard of, however. In 1913 a St. Louis woman named Pearl Curran, working through the means of a Ouija board, felt that she was being contacted by the spirit of a long-dead Puritan girl named Patience Worth. Finding communication through a Ouija board (which we will discuss later) ponderous, eventually the entity had Mrs. Curran abandon the device and take pen in hand, which permitted for a much more rapid and precise form of communication, all of which Mrs. Curran dutifully recorded over a period of several years. As it turns out, it seems Miss Worth had much to say, and the resulting correspondence resulted in seven published novels and hundreds of poems that won Mrs. Curran and her "pseudonym," Patience Worth, literary accolades. It stands to this day as one of the most profound and enduring cases of long-term spirit communication on record. Whether this was a case of genuine spirit communication or the delusional fantasies of a disturbed but talented writer remains a source of debate to this day, but the fact that such a lengthy correspondence is even potentially possible remains an intriguing possibility.

While such direct correspondence may be possible, however, it seems most people will never receive such clear telepathic messages from the great beyond. That does not mean, though, that the spiritual realm doesn't have another mean of communicating with us through the context of our subconscious that may be every bit as effective and, potentially, far more common. It's called psychic dreams.

Spirit Telepathy: Speaking Through Dreams

As I alluded earlier, dreams do seem to be a more common and, potentially, favored method of communicating with the dead. What makes it especially valuable is that a person doesn't seemingly need to possess any inherent psychic abilities or heightened spiritual sensitivity to make it work. Further, it seems to possess a number of advantages over other methods, most notably being the clarity that such communication can bring and the ease with which disembodied energies apparently can communicate with the living through this method. But how does it work?

While we cannot know with any certainty, a popular theory within the paranormal community is that when we sleep, we are no longer residing within our physical bodies, but exist in a type of transitory state between the spiritual and physical realms. Many psychics and New Age philosophers maintain that during sleep the soul actually travels outside the body to rest and recharge its spiritual "batteries" for the return trip to the world of the flesh (in fact, it is suggested that this may be the reason we need to sleep, for the energy demands of living in the physical world are so extensive that the soul cannot maintain it indefinitely, resulting in the need for periodic breaks). It is during these times that the soul, though still connected to the physical body by what some call the "golden thread"—a type of ethereal lifeline or umbilical cord—is as close to the spiritual realm as it will come while still in the flesh, which, if true, should theoretically make such times ideal for spirit communication.

Of course, few of us recall dreams in which we talk with departed loved ones, so even this form of communication may be rare (or simply something that seldom attaches itself to our conscious memory). Yet it has the advantage that when it does work, it is not only utterly nonintrusive, but can be among the most comforting and personal type of communication available. (I recounted in chapter seven the story of my wife speaking at length with her departed father in a dream and the long-term impact that had on her life.) However, if such communication should be so easy to achieve, it forces us to wonder why dream communications are so apparently rare. Could it be that such direct communication might be discouraged (or even entirely forbidden) from the other side? It may be that the spiritual realm recognizes that interacting with the physical world is frequently counterproductive and may even be, in some cases, potentially detrimental, thus possibly making departed souls extremely leery of communicating with us. In effect, communication between us and the noncorporeal energies may only be done for very special reasons or only by those "lower energies" who may not care or know better. Of course, such is purely speculative, but it would account for why interdimensional communication of all types is so uncommon.

On the other hand, some have suggested that while we can and frequently do communicate with the dearly departed on an almost nightly basis, we forget the encounter when we come back to consciousness. This is done presumably as a means of keeping the two worlds apart as they are meant to be, which does make sense. After all, if we could interact so freely with the spiritual realm and retain those experiences into our conscious world, it might have profound implications for this life. Too much contact with the other side could, in essence, pollute our physical existence, thereby effectively rendering the entire "life experiment" void. We need some uncertainty about what happens to us when we die in order to pursue this life with the prerequisite amount of enthusiasm needed to get us through the daily trials and tribulations of living. As such, if we do have the ability to contact the spirit realm when we are asleep, it is best we have no of it while we are awake (unless it has some immediate ⌐r our waking existence).

Means of Non-Telepathic Spirit Communication

Telepathic communication between the world of the flesh and spirit remains probably the safest and most nonintrusive means of talking with a disembodied consciousness, but it is only one method of doing so. As mentioned earlier, there are a number of other ways spiritual entities may have of communicating with us, either through other people or through more direct, physical means. We will look at each in turn to explore how they operate and gage their usefulness as a means of spirit communication, and we will start with the most obvious, famous—and infamous—of all, the traditional seance.

The Séance

As alluded to in the opening paragraph, the séance has acquired a fairly bad reputation over the years, with stories of trickery and blatant exploitation seemingly becoming the norm rather than the exception. Perhaps no man did more to expose the lucrative and dishonest practice than famed magician Harry Houdini, who made it his life's work to sit in on séances and expose how each trick was done once the lights came up. It is fair to say that Houdini single-handedly did more to bring the entire subject of the paranormal into disrepute than almost any man before him or since, and as such he remains a champion among modern skeptics and debunkers to this day.

However, it seems disingenuous and potentially even foolish to so casually dismiss the most basic and potentially simplest form of spirit communication available to us simply because of a few charlatans and the prodigious amount of bad press they have garnered over the years. The séance has been a traditional method of communing with spiritual energy since the dawn of time and so should be considered a viable option for spirit communication today (as long as it is done carefully and only in the company of people who are honest and dedicated and, most important of all, know what they are doing). I have no doubt there are legitimate mediums out there who have and do communicate with spiritual energies using this time-honored if badly maligned process, and almost anyone can find such a person if they are willing to do the research and maintain the prerequisite amounts of objectivity and caution when doing so.

How the séance works is fairly straightforward: in the basic séance, a group of people sit in a circle holding hands[42] (usually in a well lit but not brightly lit room), while concentrating on a candle flame (not always necessary) and invoking the name of the one with whom they wish to communicate (the assumption being that disembodied personalities know their names and usually come when called). If successful, at some point the requested entity arrives and, using the hosting medium as a conduit, begins speaking through him or her, usually in a somewhat disembodied voice.

In the best examples of the process, the entity seems to be able to communicate quite clearly and often in great detail, sometimes for several minutes at a time. Normally the entity is not visible to those gathered at the séance, and since information and not entertainment is the point of the exercise, poltergeist activity is usually uncommon as well (hoaxed séances are famous for objects floating through the air and other sorts of activity). Normally, there is only the voice of the medium giving answers to questions or making otherworldly statements, and such communications are usually very short-lived due to the supposed amounts of energy required to maintain the link. In many cases, the event will leave the medium fatigued or even exhausted, and it can take days for the individual to recover.

But is this genuine communication between two worlds? In other words, is the séance for real? Obviously, it should be reasonably easy for a clever and well-trained hoaxer to fake the whole event, which is why

---

42. It is usually imagined that an entity utilizes the energy of the people present to assist in its manifestation, without which it would, presumably, have a more difficult time making an appearance.

one needs to be especially careful in locating a qualified and credible medium. Additionally, other things can be done to ensure no trickery is afoot, such as keeping the lights on, holding the séance on neutral ground, or attempting to acquire some kind of verifiable information from the entity the medium would be unlikely to either possess or be able to easily guess. If some basic precautions are taken, however, and the participants are emotionally mature and especially alert, there is no valid reason why communication with a spirit via a séance shouldn't be at least theoretically possible. If there are such things as ghosts and they are desirous of communicating with the living, it seems that a séance should be as legitimate a means of achieving that goal as any other. Clearly some remarkable results have come from such meetings (which usually receive far less press than those séances that are exposed as fakes) so it has to at least be considered a possibility.

Unfortunately, even if the traditional séance might prove to be a legitimate means of communicating with the dead, it is probably not a realistic option for most people. It takes some effort to locate a qualified medium and then entice enough friends or acquaintances to give it a try, and so it is a method that can usually only be pursued with a great deal of determination. Additionally, it can become expensive, both in terms of cost and time. (Mediums deserve to be paid for their services every bit as much as a chiropractor, hypnotherapist, or marriage counselor does, as long as the price is not unreasonable. Many mediums, however, consider their abilities a god-given gift and have been known to provide their services at no cost.)

This leads some to wonder, however, if one might not be able to do a solo séance; that is, simply sit alone in a quiet room and ask an entity to make itself known, much as would be done in the traditional séance. While theoretically possible, it would probably be a waste of time. First, unless one was a medium themselves, it is uncertain how an entity might make itself known. You may simply not possess the necessary skills to make a manifestation possible. Second, such a situation seems a particularly ripe opportunity for the imagination to run wild and could well leave one badly frightened if they don't know what they're doing. Few people have the nerves to interact with the spiritual realm without considerable practice, making the novice especially susceptible to frightening themselves. People can imagine all sorts of noises and shadows when in a heightened state of fear, which can cause emotional damage in some easily frightened and overimaginative individuals. Further, can anyone really be prepared for the sudden manifestation of an otherworldly entity appearing before them, and what does one do if something does manifest itself? Without witnesses, it simply becomes a story as opposed to a traditional séance in which there are multiple witnesses. And, finally, in playing with invisible energies, one could expose themselves to other, less benign energies. As we discussed in chapter eight, there may well be such things as mischievous or even malicious entities who could take such an opportunity to do some real emotional damage. As such, one is better to stick with more traditional approaches to spirit communication than to try it on one's own, especially if he or she is a novice and is merely doing it out of curiosity.

So if the séance often proves problematic for most people, what other means might the spiritual realm have for contacting us and, more importantly, how useful might they be in achieving that? Next on the list is the infamous Ouija board.

Ouija Boards

While derided as a simple parlor trick and generally rejected by the paranormal investigator as a legitimate means of spirit communication, the Ouija board has been recorded as producing some startling results and so is worthy of at least consideration as a tool for communicating with spirits. After all, we can never be certain what method a disembodied personality might be prepared to use in its effort to communicate with us, and so the idea that a primitive or desperate entity might be willing to use the much maligned Ouija board must be taken seriously. To do otherwise and dismiss the possibility outright would be disingenuous and less than useful in considering all aspects of what might be possible with regard to spirit communication.

For those unfamiliar with the device, the Ouija is a board game in which players lightly rest their fingertips on a kidney-shaped plastic planchette as it races around a wooden board inscribed with numbers and letters, answering "yes" and "no" questions or spelling out simple words. The theory is that the invoked spiritual entity, empowered by the energy of the living, is able to use their energy to push the planchette around the board (often at remarkable speed) and so communicate through this rather labor-intensive and ponderous method. It's also important to recognize that the Ouija board is the modern equivalent of an older technique that has been used for over a century. In the original version, participants used a water glass on a tabletop that had letters and numbers fixed to it instead of a planchette and board, but it essentially worked the same way—and usually produced similar results.

Normally explained away as the simple ramblings of the board's participants inadvertently moving the device through subtle and largely unconscious muscular movements in the hands and arms, such a method of communication remains problematic at best, although once in a while some interesting and even inexplicable results have been recorded. Author John Fuller's 1976 bestseller *The Ghost of Flight 401* made reference to the use of Ouija board in an effort to contact the ghost of one of the crew members who had died onboard an American Airlines plane that crashed near Miami in 1971. Both to Mr. Fuller's and his partner's surprise, the board actually yielded a number of pertinent and later verifiable pieces of information about the mysterious crash and appeared to be the source of much of the information recorded in his book. Though one could always question Mr. Fuller's methodology, no one could question his veracity as an award-winning journalist and competent researcher (who started out as something of a skeptic in the first place), which should give the objective researcher cause to at least ponder the possibility that an entity might well make use of such a device. Additionally, the Patience Worth case recounted earlier also started out as Ouija board communication before evolving into direct spiritual dictation, thus demonstrating that not everything that comes out of these sessions is hopeless nonsense.

While it might be tempting to simply dismiss such a device as a harmless toy and move on, however, let us consider the question of the Ouija board from the perspective of a ghost for a moment. If we can accept the possibility that the human consciousness does survive death and, further, that a disembodied personality might wish to communicate with the living but lacks the ready resources or understanding of how to do so, it seems that a Ouija board might well be a tempting option. After all, here is a device that apparently takes little energy to manipulate being operated by individuals either open to the possibility or even intent on communicating with them. One should think that such an opportunity would be hard to pass up, especially for an entity desperate to make itself known.

However, a few words of caution are in order. First, one would be prudent to recognize that most of what comes from such a device is likely going to be largely a product of the imagination, and so everything should be taken with a very large grain of salt. Second, it should be remembered that people have been badly frightened by such devices, so its use should never be attempted by those who are easily traumatized, emotionally immature, or psychologically unstable. Third, any useful information gleaned from such a device is probably going to be acquired only through many hours of tedious and slow-paced work, making it a ponderous process that is unlikely to prove particularly useful in the long run. As such, if individuals believe they are truly communicating with a spiritual entity through such a device, they would be wise to seek the services of a reputable medium if they want to pursue the contact further.

Finally, there is one more point to consider. Such a device, assuming it can be a genuine conduit for spiritual entities to communicate with the living, could also open the gate to malevolent or primitive entities to come through, and since we do not have a clear understanding of how such entities might choose to interact within our physical realm or how they might affect us on an emotional or psychological level, inadvertently inviting them into one's world would be extremely unwise. Malevolent entities seem to work on a "lesser" energy level, and if the Ouija board potentially empowers such energies, they could well be attracted to such a device and prove to be a real problem if they were to make use of it. As such, using Ouija board to communicate with the dead should be used only as a last resort (if ever), at least until such time as we better understand precisely how it works and what it can do.

Channeled and Automatic Writing

The idea that spiritual energies might make direct use of a willing host's motor functions in an effort to communicate is another intriguing possibility. Known as "spirit writing," such potential communication is both a fascinating and largely under-reported phenomena that holds out considerable possibilities if spirit communication is ever to become a reality.

Spirit writing comes in two forms. In the first, known as "channeling," a spirit allegedly has a willing host essentially transcribe what it wishes to communicate directly onto paper, much as a secretary taking dictation would do. (This was the process by which the alleged ghost Patience Worth wrote her stories through Mrs. Curran.) With this method, the host is "inspired" or otherwise compelled to record various thoughts or ideas onto paper—thoughts that appear to be originating outside themselves and which they do their best to accurately record. In some cases, the host or channeler is directly instructed to record what they are told by the entity and may spend months or even many years dutifully recording these thoughts and bringing them into some sort of comprehensive form. The end result, then, is a collaboration between entity and host, with the writing being a conglomeration of writing styles and ideas.

The second method, known as "automatic" writing, is similar in that it is the recording of an entity's thoughts, but in this case the entity itself actually takes over a person's motor skills and records its thoughts directly onto paper. Essentially, a willing host simply holds pen to paper and waits for "something" to move the device—not unlike waiting for the planchette on the Ouija board to begin to move—which then proceeds to produce coherent, legible statements.[43] It is as if their hand has been surrendered to the entity, which is in effect "borrowing" their motor functions in an effort to make itself known, often with amazing results. Additionally, unlike inspired or channeled writing, the host does not process in their brain what is being written and can even be entirely distracted during the process, making the human agent almost unnecessary. In most cases, they don't know themselves what is being written and only learn what they have penned afterward, once they have had a chance to go over the material.

Channeled writing is probably the more prevalent and better known phenomena of the two methods, with a number of New Age books having been allegedly written in this manner. Among the earliest and perhaps best known of the channeled books (unless one is prepared to include the Bible, the Koran, and other traditional religious texts in this group) is the Seth series, written by California writer Jane Roberts starting in 1963 and ending with her death in 1984. Ms. Robert's books became especially popular in the late 1970s and proved to be instrumental in introducing the entire issue of channeled writing into the public consciousness. Writing from the persona of an entity she knew simply as Seth and usually while in a trance-like state, Ms. Roberts went on to pen over twenty books by or about Seth and his teachings, with seven of them being allegedly directly channeled by Seth personally. While generally panned by the scientific community, it has proven to be an especially compelling and interesting body of work that has survived its critics' best efforts at downplaying the phenomenon, and most of her books remain in print even today.

---

43. Modern automatic writers have taken to using the computer rather than paper by letting their fingers rest lightly on a keyboard and then allowing the entity to type in their stead. Though often just as interesting, it is less conclusive than handwritten automatic text that can be more easily compared and studied for style and form.

Other well-known channeled books include *A Course in Miracles* (perhaps one of most complex and sophisticated of the genre) and the *Conversations with God* series penned by Oregonian writer Neale Donald Walsch.[44] These books differ from the Seth series, however, in that they portend to be conversations not with some disembodied personality, but with God itself (or, in the case of the *Miracles* discourses, with Jesus), further "upping the ante" within the paranormal community. Whether one believes these individuals are genuinely in contact with some external force or the writings are all the work of overactive imaginations, however, it is an incontrovertible fact that such material has frequently proven to contain remarkably sophisticated and even life-changing ideas, thoughts, and theories generally considered beyond the intellectual and spiritual understanding of their authors. Whether this would constitute true spirit communication can only be guessed at, but that it has produced some impressive results cannot be denied and is deserving of serious consideration.

In contrast to channeled writing, automatic writing is a far less common form of spirit communication. However, like channeled material, it too can occasionally produce some astonishing results. Perhaps the most remarkable are the handful of cases in which the entity identifies itself by name, thus allowing investigators to compare the final written script with existing handwriting samples of the individual it claimed to be. On occasion, these prove not only to be identical in writing style and script, but in vocabulary, punctuation, and even nuance as well—something that would be extremely difficult to fake.[45] While not proof of supernatural contact, it remains among the best evidence to date that the dead not only can contact us, but that they retain an extraordinary amount of their previous personality even in the spirit realm.

---

44. There is some debate as to whether Walsch's writings technically qualify as channeled material since much in his books is written in his own words, as opposed to most channeled writing that is usually recorded verbatim with no input from the author. If true, this would make Walsch's books more akin to inspired rather than channeled writing.

45. An excellent example of this is the case of Grace Rosher as recorded in *Spirits and the Spirit Worlds*, by Roy Stemman (Doubleday & Co., 1975), pp. 90–91.

Both types of phenomena have been hotly debated and carefully studied within the parapsychology community for decades with no final verdict being reached. Not surprisingly, in most scientific circles the entire notion of both automatic and channeled writing is routinely dismissed as nothing more than another demonstration of the power of the mind to manifest a subconsciously induced fantasy, but then that is empirical science's answer to almost everything having to do with the paranormal.

So what are we to make of these phenomena? That they may yet prove to be a legitimate means of spirit communication seems possible, but that there is not enough solid evidence to prove anything either way is also a fact. It is also not clear whether, assuming they are a genuine means of contacting disembodied energies, anyone can use them or if they are available only to a gifted few. Most likely, like the Ouija board, it is something that one would need to experiment with before making a decision. A very careful examination of the final product should be made before accepting anything at face value. However, if entities are intent on communicating with us, this would appear to be an efficient means of doing so, and so it does seem to show some promise as a legitimate means of spirit communication. However, also like the Ouija board, if legitimate it too could potentially serve as a conduit for primitive or malevolent entities to make themselves known, so channeling and the use of automatic writing should be approached with considerable caution as well.

Speaking with the Dead

While Ouija boards and automatic writing are interesting phenomena to consider, it seems that what we are really looking for is a more basic, simpler method of talking with the departed that does not involve props and endless hours of meditation and transcribing. In other words, we want a means by which we might speak with ghosts easily and in an ongoing, consistent manner, much as we would with the still living. Such, however, appears extremely difficult to accomplish.

Or is it? Certainly, some people have reported considerable success simply vocalizing to ghosts and getting them to respond in various ways (such as rapping on walls, tipping tables, or responding to some specific request). Usually such communications have to do with requests to leave or questions about what the entity wants, but the fact that ghosts have been reported to respond to such statements is significant. They may not be capable of answering us verbally or audibly, but that does not mean we lack the ability to be understood by these beings. In fact, ghosts may be more capable of understanding us than we imagine.

However, even if they are capable of understanding us, does that mean we should pursue opportunities to speak to them? There are a couple of schools of thought on this. Some maintain that since ghosts are the residual energy of human personalities that refuse to move on to the spiritual realm so they can continue their spiritual journey, it suggests that there could be something wrong with them, in which case it would be unwise to engage them directly. With the exception of those familials who wish to provide a last word of comfort to the bereaved or mission ghosts who have some vital unfinished business to take care of before they can move on, most ghosts may simply be souls who are lost on this plane of existence and so are likely to have little of value to say to us in any case. Most are wandering and confused spirits trying to find their way home, so communicating with any of them, except perhaps for the purpose of encouraging them to find their way back to the light, is probably counterproductive and may, in some cases, even be dangerous. Therefore, if you should happen to find yourself in a position of being in the clear presence of a ghost, your best bet may be to simply say nothing to it.

Another belief, however, maintains that since ghosts are the residual energy of human beings like ourselves, engaging them is unlikely to be any more dangerous than would be striking up a conversation with a stranger one has just met. Additionally, it seems that the chance to learn something about the next world firsthand would be too good an opportunity to pass up, and so the idea of remaining silent might be easily construed as a tragically missed opportunity. After all, who better to ask about the afterlife than a ghost?

Interesting point, but then it presumes that the dead have all the answers we seek, which is not necessarily a good bet. Chances are that most ghosts don't know any more about what's happening to them than we do, which is probably the reason they are a ghost in the first place. The idea that dear old Aunt Edna suddenly becomes an oracle of wisdom and knowledge just because she is now dead is presumptuous; more likely she is still the same confused but lovable lady you knew in life, only now she may be even more confused than before. Therefore, engaging spirits in some metaphysical discussion—while a powerful temptation—is probably going to prove a waste of time.

For those who still wish to pursue contact, however, a few words of caution are in order, however. It is probably not a good idea to shout at a ghost, call it names, or attempt to "cast it out." If it is an angry ghost, that may just provoke it into violence (much as it would a living person), and I would imagine few ghosts would appreciate being looked upon as an "unclean spirit" requiring the services of an exorcist. Further, some ghosts may be as frightened of us as we are of them, so it seems cruel to verbally assault them. Probably the best advice, assuming you're up to saying anything to a ghost at all, is to simply—and gently—remind it that it is dead and urge it to move on. Chances are they already know this—at least on some level—and your encouragement may be just enough incentive to get them to trust the process and proceed to the spirit realm. It's usually not that easy, but such admonishments have been reported to occasionally work.

This might work for the ghost of a stranger, but what of our loved ones who have since passed on? What if we want—or need—to speak with them, perhaps for our own assurance that they are well and to tell them how much we miss and love them? Is that a good idea, or should we instead ignore them and go on with our own lives, content in the fact that we will see them someday once our own life here on Earth is finished?

It really depends on the person. Some people have an extremely difficult time letting go of loved ones, and so it seems there are circumstances in which attempting to speak to the spirit of a departed spouse or family member might be helpful and even, potentially, cathartic. Likely the departed loved one also understands this and is doing their best to assist the grieving process along before moving on. In this case, the best response to them might be just a simple "I love you and miss you. Thanks for letting me know you're all right," which will usually be enough to get them on their way. For other people, however, such a visitation can be quite unsettling and probably counterproductive; a possibility it is hoped the departed loved one also understands and would be careful to avoid.

Conclusion

In the end, I believe the souls of the departed are still interested in our world, still concerned with what's happening here on Earth, and, in many cases, still vitally involved in our day-to-day existence. Further, I am convinced, especially in the case of family and friends who have passed, that they also weep with us, continue to encourage us, watch over us, and, in their own subtle and gentle ways, continue to let us know they are here long after they have left their material bodies.

If true, that suggests we should be able to communicate with them whenever we wish, not through mediums or Ouija boards or some other mechanism, but through the voice of love. And, if our personalities do continue to exist after we are gone and if we are still able to sense and feel and be aware from the other side just as we are on this side, we should be able to hear each other across the expanse of time and space as clearly as we do now. As such, communicating with our loved ones, or with any spiritual entity for that matter, may be no more difficult than simply speaking to them in our hearts. I believe the messages, especially those of love (which is, after all, the most powerful and pervasive energy in the universe), will be easily received by those we need to hear it. They may not be able to reciprocate those messages as they could in the flesh, but even one-way communication is still communication after all, and even that will be enough to allow us to remain a part of them.

Additionally, how do we know they may not have other, more subtle, ways of responding to us that we are not aware of? Accounts of people sensing the presence of a passed loved one, especially during times of great sadness or distress, are common, so we should keep ourselves open to feeling their energy when they come into our presence.[46] After all, the universe is a very big place, and, as we understand so little about what makes it function, the thought that love forms a bond between two worlds that even death cannot break is not so hard to imagine. It is all simply a matter of faith, which, in the end, may be all that really exists in the world of the infinite.

---

46. The fact that we can sense the presence of loved ones should not be taken to mean they are necessarily a ghost. They may simply be reaching out from their world to our own to let us know they are still around and thinking of us.

chapter thirteen

Spirit Guides

Do you have a spirit guide? Millions of people believe they do. In fact, the idea that we have a spirit guide (also known in some traditions as a spirit master, counselor, or guardian angel) personally assigned to each one of us is as old as the belief in ghosts and is a major element of New Age teachings (as well as a part of some traditional religious beliefs as well).[47] However, the concept has proven to be an increasingly contentious point of debate within the paranormal field—as well as among the most problematic—that requires some serious consideration.

Before starting, however, let me go on record as saying that I have never been a big proponent of the idea that we each have our own individual spiritual entity (or guardian angel) watching over us to protect us from harm. Such an idea, no matter how innocently maintained, strikes me as little more than superstition. For too many people, such a being seems to function almost as a type of invisible bodyguard or a sort of magical genie who will make life run a little smoother. While probably harmless, taking such a belief to the extreme seems to me a recipe for disaster, especially if it causes one to look for things outside themselves to make them feel happy, safe, or secure. We should not be dependent upon some entity or angel to get

---

47. Catholicism and some branches of evangelical Christianity, for example, maintain a belief in these higher beings, though they are almost always referred to as guardian angels or the "Holy Spirit" rather than spirit guides. They serve essentially the same purpose, however.

us through the rough patches of life, for in doing so we run the risk of retarding our own spiritual development by turning over the responsibilities of overcoming the challenges and trials of life to some higher power. Additionally, it also allows us to shift the blame when things go wrong to some external force who "let us down" rather than looking within ourselves and examining our own actions—or lack thereof—for the cause of our problems. It is always easier to count on and blame others than it is to take responsibility for our own life, potentially making the belief in guardian angels or spirit guides a detriment to spiritual growth rather than an aide to it.

On the other hand, in chapter three we discussed the possibility and, in fact, the probability of nonhuman entities existing within the universe (those I referred to as extra-celestials) and that these entities may be both willing and quite able to interact with us, not as personal bodyguards or magic elves, but as conduits to greater universal knowledge and wisdom. These beings are not ghosts in the normal sense of the word, nor are they disembodied personalities of once living people. Instead, they are beings that have always existed within a spiritual context and have a much broader, far more grandiose agenda in mind beyond keeping us safe and comfortable. Their goal is to work on our individual and collective spiritual natures in an effort to bring us to ever greater levels of personal and societal maturity, which they do by planting the seeds that will germinate into ideas and philosophies that will eventually fuel great advances in human understanding and knowledge. In effect, they work for humanity's betterment behind the scenes in subtle ways, moving us along our spiritual journey toward ever grander vistas of understanding and enlightenment, all in an effort to bring greater unity and cohesion to the divine essence that permeates the universe. It has to be more than a byproduct of evolutionary genetics or the result of pure, dumb luck that we have managed the journey from simple, cave-dwelling primates to creatures capable of art, literature, science, and even complex philosophies like democracy and inherent human rights. Despite our frequent setbacks and tremendous capacity for foolishness and brutality, we have somehow still managed to come a remarkable distance in a comparatively short time (at least in terms of recent Earth history), which leads me to wonder if some of our greatest steps forward as a species haven't been, at least in part, a result of the work of these highly advanced and evolved spiritual beings working through the minds and hearts of some of our planet's greatest thinkers, philosophers, leaders, and teachers throughout history. I think it significant that many of the great spiritual masters and religious leaders of the past have attributed their teachings to wisdom they acquired from precisely such spiritual agents, and so we should be open to at least the possibility that such beings are at work in our world even today. It simply doesn't follow that these entities might have instilled knowledge and guidance in a Socrates, a Buddha, a Krishna, or a Gandhi and then decided they have no interest in continuing with the process—especially at a time when we as a species both show such promise and are in such grave danger at the same time. It is almost impossible to imagine that they would not want to continue the process, and so it is not unreasonable to imagine such entities might well be available and willing to communicate with those who truly seek them out today.

That, however, should not be taken to suggest that such beings only interact with the most powerful, most educated, and most famous among us; tremendous spiritual movements have been begun by very ordinary people who simply happened to have the heart for the message that was implanted in them. A good example of this can be seen in the man we call Jesus of Nazareth. Despite coming from uneducated and common stock, he started a movement fairly late in his life that was to sweep the known world with its message of peace and love until, in a few short centuries, the religion we know today as Christianity conquered an empire. Could the source of much of his knowledge and wisdom have been given to him by advanced spiritual entities intent on pulling the world out of its darkness? The gospel accounts themselves write of Jesus spending considerable time alone in quiet meditation; could that have been when he communed with the higher energies of the universe and recharged his spiritual batteries for the task set before him? Such is a provocative possibility that needs to be considered.

Of course, not everyone is being tapped to become the next Jesus or Buddha or Gandhi. More likely there are many people interacting with these spiritual entities—either consciously or unconsciously— every day, acquiring small bits of wisdom as they require it and are able to receive it, which they will then weave into the greater mosaic of human evolution and spiritual development through their actions and deeds. It is also my belief that enlightenment and understanding is much more of a collective effort today than it has been in the past, when the pool of potential students was far smaller. Whereas in centuries past only a handful of individuals were capable of tuning into these spiritual entities because of the generally low level of human spiritual awareness, as we evolved as a species more and more people became aware of and capable of interacting with these beings until today perhaps millions are capable of doing so, making the pool of those who may have access to such beings considerable. This means that almost anyone who is open to the possibility that such entities exist and is desirous of contacting one for the purpose of developing themselves spiritually should be able to—at least in theory—tap into the "universal consciousness" from which these beings operate and develop a relationship.

That being said, however, while I don't believe such entities play favorites, I do suspect they are more likely to seek out—or at least respond to—certain individuals more than others. It makes sense that if an advanced, enlightened entity were intent on advancing human understanding or growing us spiritually on an individual level, it would be more likely to interact with those who are sincere and truly desirous of growing spiritually than they would with someone who was merely "playing" with the supernatural. This is an area ripe for fraud, manipulation, and self-deception by people who are not spiritually mature enough to genuinely maintain such a relationship. Some have even taken to manufacturing "spirit guides" out of their own imagination because it feeds their ego-driven need to feel safe, important, or powerful, thus undermining the entire field of spirit communication and making it rife with counterfeits. In essence, spirit guides aren't for everyone, but only for those who are truly ready to receive them.

Therefore, if highly evolved spiritual masters intervene at all, I suspect they are much more likely to plant their seeds of wisdom where they will bear fruit rather than scatter them to the four winds, so one needs to examine one's own motives and sincerity in developing such a relationship. I am convinced these entities know who is ready and able to handle their tutelage and who is not, and they respond only to those who honestly pursue them and are entirely devoid of any agenda beyond the desire to grow spiritually or help humanity.

Before moving on, it is first necessary to better define exactly what is meant by a spirit guide and, further, how it is distinguished from our own subconscious or "inner self." To answer that, it is first necessary to understand how our own psyche works to some degree, which can only be accomplished by examining what our "inner" or "higher" self is and how it operates.

Distinguishing the "Higher Self" from a Spirit Master

There is a belief within psychology that there exists within all human beings an inherent ethical nature or "voice" built directly into the human psyche whose function seems to be to serve as a type of self-correcting mechanism. This internal resource is basically responsible for protecting us from harm and, among other things, helping us maintain a proper and balanced sense of reality lest we stray too far from sound mental health. As such, when we feel depressed to the point of being suicidal or become over-anxious, fearful, or nervous to a degree that our health is suffering, it is this "higher self" that intervenes to encourage us to seek help or, at the very least, help us recognize that a problem exists. Additionally, when we feel guilt or shame at betraying some personal moral edict, that too is often our higher self speaking to us, attempting to keep us from wandering too far into a moral or ethical quagmire of our own making. The higher self, then, serves as a kind of moral compass designed to maintain humanity's inherent sense of ethics and morality, in which case its "voice" can be most closely equated with our conscience.

Some see it in slightly different ways, however. Western religion tends to see this inner mechanism more as a force designed to protect us from sinning rather than as a purely emotional and psychological healing mechanism (though, of course, it might adequately serve both functions simultaneously), while Eastern and New Age concepts see it as neither a "sin shield" nor a self-preservation mechanism, but purely as a device designed to push us toward greater spiritual growth. In this, the "higher self" is seen as the immortal, divine part of ourselves—the true soul—as opposed to the temporal, ego part that we normally call the personality—and that it is working tirelessly to bring us to spiritual maturation in much the same way a parent might push a lazy child through school.

Regardless of how one chooses to interpret this internal mechanism, however, the point is that it is not the same thing as a spirit guide, for our "higher self" is not something external to us, but an integral part of ourselves that operates within the deepest realms of our subconscious and is primarily concerned with the self. Additionally, it is somewhat limited in its ability to move us toward spiritual maturation (though it can still be extremely important to our development and well-being) and often can be little more than a reflection of our already existent spiritual state rather than a mechanism for future growth.

Unfortunately, this "little voice in our head" can be easily mistaken for the voice of a spirit guide, so how do we know when the information we receive is originating internally within ourselves or is from some external source?

It is not always easy to tell the difference, but I find that there is a fundamental difference: the higher self or "internal guidance mechanism" is chiefly interested in the self while the "spirit guide" is primarily concerned with bringing us to a point where we can be of use to others. In other words, the "inner voice" is essentially self-serving while the "outer voice" is designed to serve others. Of course, the very process of spiritual maturation itself will eventually bring one to a point of selflessness, but this is usually the byproduct of a very long process (and, potentially, the end result only of many lifetimes). These spiritual entities, in contrast, are here to "speed things up" by making participants a tool for greater social change even if they are not entirely spiritually mature themselves (which is why most of the great thinkers and philosophers of history have demonstrated serious flaws in other areas of their lives). In other words, they are attracted to people who merely show potential even if they do not have their entire act together yet.

Additionally, while we may all have this internal self-correcting/spiritually maturing mechanism built into our very DNA, spirit guides have to be invited into our lives. They do not force themselves upon a person and will leave whenever requested to do so.[48] Also, a spirit guide operates differently than does the inner-self mechanism. The inner sense works more behind the scenes through the subtle mechanism of intuition, urgings, and impressions, while a true guide is much more external and overt and more akin to someone standing over your shoulder feeding you helpful ideas or insights. It can often be conversational (or even "chatty") in nature, making it more personable and intimate than might be possible with the inner self.

By way of an example, suppose you are anxious or depressed and are having trouble sleeping at night. The higher self in this instance will give you a sense that all is not well and instill within you the impression that you would be wise to seek medical or psychological help. The guide, in contrast, is more likely to suggest a specific book to read or person you might talk with about the problem; in essence, a guide is more specific in its advice while the higher-self mechanism tends to be more general in nature. That, at least, is my impression of how the two elements work, though, of course, I am open to the notion

---

48. If they don't, you are more likely dealing with a malevolent or mischievous entity masquerading as a spirit guide rather than a genuine spirit master. Normally, such entities cannot keep up the charade up for long and will inevitably reveal themselves for what they are, at which point it may be necessary to insist that they leave. In fact, a true spirit guide may be able to help you drive them out.

that yours may well operate differently. The only point I'm trying to make here is that they do not, at least in my experiences, function in the same way and that there are very distinct and, in some cases, even profound differences between them. As such, you should be able to distinguish between your higher self and a spirit guide relatively easily, especially after you have worked with a guide for awhile.

Spirit Guide or God?

Before moving on, it is my experience that many people are uncomfortable with the idea that there exists around us a world of invisible beings with whom we may converse and receive guidance. To many raised in a Judeo-Christian environment, it smacks of the occult, which has always been considered a forbidden realm of endeavor for purveyors of Western religion. Even among those who believe that they have a guardian angel, there is a hesitancy to attempt to contact it directly. To some, it is believed that communicating with these divine messengers might be an affront to God, who is normally considered the only supernatural being acceptable for a Christian, Jew, or Muslim to contact directly (in fact, it is encouraged). And this can be a valid concern for many. After all, if you define God as the master spirit being from whom all other spirit beings arose, then doing an "end run" around him might be something of a problem (especially if you consider him a jealous and easily offended God as most Western religions—and many evangelical Christians—contend). This is the reason why they generally discourage their adherents from attempting to contact angels directly.[49]

If, on the other hand, you see God as a pervasive eternal spirit that is the essence of all that is, then the idea that you can contact any single facet of this force should be considered both reasonable and even logical. For that matter, it might even be argued that contacting these higher energies is the only way to connect with God, for the divine is

---

49. Of course, there are those Christians who do not believe that God has any objections to our contacting other spiritual agents (as long as they are "good" ones) or, for that matter, even the spirits of the dead, but that is the minority view. Generally, communication with any entity other than God, Jesus, or the Holy Spirit is expressly forbidden.

too vast and nonlinear to be perceived or comprehended any other way. In other words, to contact one's spirit guide is to be in communication with God—the one being synonymous with the other.

As for myself, I tend toward the view that God is simply another term for the collective energy and knowledge of the universe, and therefore I see a spirit guide as a conduit—or tap—from which to access this universal force. I differentiate this force from ghosts, however, which I perceive to be separate, individualized expressions of this greater force that are largely disconnected from it (which is the main reason ghosts do not seem to be particularly knowledgeable about the spiritual realm).

Whichever definition of God one chooses is, of course, left entirely up to the reader. All I can say is that whether you feel comfortable with the notion of communicating with advanced supernatural entities will most likely be determined by how you define the term God. If one maintains a traditional, Western perspective, it may prove almost impossible to feel comfortable about accessing a spirit guide, whereas someone who maintains an Eastern perspective of the divine may find it considerably easier to do so. It really is all a matter of one's personal perspective and individual comfort level.

In the end, if you are leery of attempting to communicate with a spirit guide, you are probably better off not to try it. It is not essential for spiritual evolution to take place (which is generally realized through the day-to-day trials, triumphs, and tribulations of life), so one who is not entirely comfortable with the notion is most likely better off without it. In fact, if you feel more comfortable praying to God rather than seeking out a spirit guide, you are probably better off to continue with that. It is not easy to alter a lifetime of religious training and beliefs, so if you are not open to it, don't try it.

Speaking with Your Guide

If we work from the premise that such beings that we refer to as spirit guides truly do exist and that they are open to and even desirous of communicating with us, it would follow that attempting to communicate with them is a good idea. In fact, there are those who suggest that since a spirit guide is a higher spiritual energy whose purpose is to oversee our spiritual evolution, frequent communication with it would not only be useful but might prove invaluable in maintaining our spiritual and emotional health. But how do we initiate this contact? Where do we start?

The first thing we must accept is that these beings really are willing and able to interact with us. After all, if the spirits of human beings have shown a willingness to communicate with us, it seems disingenuous to discount the possibility that nonhuman spiritual beings may wish to do the same and, further, if they did, that they would not have a superior means of doing so. In fact, such beings, perhaps having always existed in a spiritual state, should be in a better position to know all the "tricks" of interacting within the realm of linear time and space than even the most seasoned human ghost, and so they should have a fairly easy time of making themselves heard. As such, the first thing we must accept is that it *can* be done.

Second, it is essential to embrace the idea that these agents are desirous of interacting with us personally. The biggest obstacle most people have to overcome is learning to accept the idea that they are "worthy" of having a spirit guide and that these beings are not just for "holy people" or men and women of great faith and moral purity. Spirit guides do not judge us and would, in fact, consider anyone who is genuine and honest in their quest to be worthy. Spirit guides are not for special people, but for ordinary people like you and I.

Once one is convinced that such communication is both possible and beneficial, it might be helpful to first read a few books on the subject of spirit guides until one feels they understand the concept pretty well. The best way to do this is compare authors and look for the common threads that tie their teachings together. This is usually sufficient to keep one from turning any single author into an "infallible" source of information and so fall into potential error and spiritual wanderings. Then, once one is completely comfortable with the idea that these beings are accessible and willing to communicate with them, the best thing to do is simply clear one's mind and open themselves to their presence and wait. Getting away from life's distractions, such as going for a walk in a deserted park or meditating in a quiet room in your home, is practically imperative. Additionally, ensure that you are not upset, angry, frustrated, or distracted at the time. Though guides can still respond when you are feeling strong negative emotions, it has been my experience that they are sometimes harder to perceive during such times. Meditation is a good way to purge oneself of such emotions and make oneself more "in tune" with the spiritual realm. Also, some people find staring at a candle flame to be a good way of making themselves sensitive to these external energies, though I have not personally found either discipline particularly useful (although I can appreciate how either would help clear one's mind of the clutter of day-to-day living). Just use whatever works best for you.

Since it is frequently difficult for human beings to comprehend or maintain an image of an invisible being for any length of time, it may be necessary to create a mental picture in your mind to assist in making communication with these entities easier. For example, when I first began my correspondence, it was frequently necessary for me to visualize myself talking with another person. Being a Christian when I first began this communication, I considered this make-believe entity to be God and even endowed "Him" with a specific physical appearance, manner of speaking, and even a sense of humor. In fact, since many people find the thought of communicating with a spirit guide to be a bit spooky, you might find it easier to imagine yourself talking with God instead. This, in effect, makes such communication more akin to meditative prayer, which is usually considered more socially acceptable and won't get you in trouble at your church, synagogue, or mosque. Of course, a part of me knew this was all a construct of my imagination, but it served to help me focus my thoughts and made it easier for me to pick up what it was I believe "He" (and like most Christians, I tended to picture God as a male) was saying to me.

As I moved along in my understanding, however, eventually I was able to discard the image I had created. Apparently, "it" simply used the vehicle I had created and then discarded it once I no longer required it. Now I envision myself speaking more with a friend walking alongside me, which I find less intimidating and more agreeable to pursuing a give-and-take dialogue. This demonstrates how useful and, indeed, invaluable is the role the imagination plays in this process.

The Role of the Imagination

The ability to imagine things is largely an unappreciated tool for spiritual development. In fact, it is those who consider the imagination the source of all deceit and so refuse to use it that forever cut themselves off from the source of all wisdom and knowledge. This is because most people equate the use of the imagination with "making things up," and so they fail to see it for what it is: the gift of the divine designed to help us visualize that which exists outside ourselves so that we may acquire some means of comprehending it. It is a byproduct of sentience instilled within us that makes spiritual progress even possible, for without it we should forever be limited to what reality we can perceive with our five natural senses. The supernatural largely exists outside the physical realm, and it is our ability to imagine it—that is, "image it"—that opens the door to that realm.

Of course, the imagination, when undisciplined and given free reign in our lives, can lead to all sorts of problems, so caution is in order. However, when used in conjunction with our rational senses, it is the key to spiritual growth. Without it, I could never have imagined myself speaking with God or talking with a spirit guide the way one would talk with a friend. Obviously, these mental pictures I create are not what these entities actually appear as, for they exist in a state of pure energy and so have no recognizable form that we might perceive. However, in imagining what they look or sound like, I create a conduit between my world and theirs that makes communication possible.

Further, the imagination is more than a spiritual tool, but is eminently practical in daily living as well. Consider for a moment how chaotic our lives would be if we lacked the imagination to consider how our plans might work out under various scenarios. Nothing could be invented, designed, or even built without the imagination first envisioning the product in the mind's eye and then testing every conceivable circumstance under which that product will be used. It is not only what gives us the ability to create, but even affords us the means to live a fulfilled life. While it can also get us in trouble—especially when it is integrated with fear—it is also that which can get us out of trouble, if used correctly and wisely.

As such, do not be afraid to use your imagination in this process. Just remember that the images you receive are just that: images. They are not to be confused with absolute reality. They are symbols of a deeper and greater truth that lies buried deep within the recesses of your mind, but only symbols of that truth. Once you become comfortable with that and understand the vitally important role the imagination plays in all this, you will be better prepared to enter into an intensely personal and unique relationship with the supernatural that will bring many benefits to your life.

Listening for the Voice

Once you have reached a state where you feel open, relaxed, and comfortable about continuing, begin asking questions—usually silently to yourself (though they can also be spoken out loud)—or let your mind wander over some event or situation you are concerned about. Perhaps make a few observations, pose a few questions—and wait. And listen.

Eventually you should have a sensation that "something" is answering you. It will not be an audible voice[50] but more of an impression. It may even sound like your own voice answering your query, making you suspect that you are making the whole thing up, which is okay. Go with that and let this "fictional" two-way conversation flow. That is why we have an imagination—as a means of helping us get started. Eventually, however, as you grow more comfortable with the dialogue, you will start to feel like you are actually talking to someone outside yourself and any artificial qualities the conversation possessed initially will soon begin to fade.

So how do you know if you are actually talking with your spirit guide? I cannot speak for others, but as for me I get a sense of peace and become aware of being immersed in an invisible cloud of tremendous knowledge, patience, and wisdom. It is a feeling of profound "oneness" that makes you feel as if you are, in effect, "home" or, more precisely, exactly where you belong. Once you come to feel you are a part of that energy and it is a part of you, you can be pretty sure you are in the presence of something larger than yourself.

But how do you know if it is just your own imagination making you feel a certain way? After all, human beings seem quite capable of deluding themselves.

Good question with no easy answer. In fact, as I alluded to a moment ago, at first it may be your own imagination in the driver's seat, so don't take everything you hear—especially in the early stages of this dialogue—as gospel truth. In other words, be as objective as you know how about what impressions you receive and do not automatically assume you are entirely connected. It is easy to fool oneself, so even a

---

50. Some people claim to actually be able to hear their spirit guide audibly, but that has never been my experience. It strikes me that since telepathic communication is so much more efficient, audible communication would seem to be both unnecessary and, potentially, even problematic. As such, I wouldn't expect to hear your spirit master audibly (though often the voice within your head can be extraordinarily clear and even "loud" in its own way). I suspect most people who claim to hear these voices on a consistent basis are either experiencing psychosomatic hallucinations or are making things up—perhaps in an effort to sound more spiritual in the presumption that audible voices are more impressive than simple internal communications. As such, if you hear actual voices, I would be suspicious and extremely wary, and would consider psychiatric counseling if they become frequent or insistent.

sprinkling of skepticism is helpful (although too much may make communication almost impossible. Balance is the key here). However, there are some clues that can help you determine whether you are in the presence of a higher energy or merely the victim of self-delusion. The best way to do this is by simply listening to the responses you receive to your questions and carefully considering the thoughts that pop into your head. Run them through your logical senses and examine whether they contain any hint of selfishness or personal ambition. For example, does the "voice" tell you to take the rent money and buy lottery tickets with it? If so, it is probably safe to ignore it. Does it tell you that affair with the attractive coworker at the office you are tempted to pursue is okay or that the company won't miss it if you abscond with one of their many laptop computers? If so, you are playing games with yourself. In other words, if what you pick up is self-serving, unusual, confusing, or just plain morally wrong, there is good reason to wonder if such musings are not more likely internally generated rather than genuine external communication (or whether you might not be picking up the musings of some malevolent energies). Also, beware of "quick and easy" answers or promises you believe your guide is making; these are more likely examples of wishful thinking rather than true spirit communication. The rule of thumb is that if your spirit guide keeps confirming or endorsing everything you already believe, it is probably just your imagination playing tricks on you. I tend to get in arguments with my "inner voice" (arguments that I usually lose), which is how I know it is unlikely to be me just pretending to be a spirit guide.

Additionally, do not expect immediate answers and spontaneous insights to suddenly flood your senses; a true spirit guide isn't keen on supplying direct answers to your every question but in getting you to find the answers within yourself. They may simply help you see a situation with renewed clarity or impress upon you an idea or insight you had not thought of before rather than directly tell you what to do. They seem to enjoy working through circumstances, curious turns of events, and other people, so look for them to suggest that you speak with a certain individual or bring to mind a book or movie that might contain the answer you seek. I can't tell you how many books I have been "led" to read that helped me considerably in my journey, demonstrating that such beings are frequently far more interested in using other humans to help us than they are in giving us the answers directly.

A few words of caution, though. It is easy to fall into the trap of thinking this entity can be turned on like a light switch whenever one desires. While my guide can talk to me at any time, I've always found that I had to make myself open or sensitive to its energy, and that often takes some work. Clearing one's mind and really concentrating is a prerequisite that is easy to overlook, resulting in a monologue being mistaken for a dialogue. In other words, it is easy to get this "being" to say whatever you want it to say if you are not careful, so people need to be especially honest with themselves if they want to pursue this. This is where the ancient art of discernment comes in; knowing when you are really on the right "wavelength" and knowing when you are not is a tool that takes years to develop, but it is a vital one to have if one is to truly tap into the universal consciousness on a consistent basis.

Of course, even after many years of doing this I still occasionally find my ego trying to assert itself, but since I know my inner voice so well I usually know what's going on and either concentrate a little harder in an effort to get back on track or give up and try another day. Just as there are times when a musician just can't seem to feel the music, it is best to recognize that our spiritual sensitivity sometimes wanes. It is easy to contact these energies if you truly want to, but sometimes you just have to admit when you are blocked and move on.

As I said, this is what I have experienced over the years. It may be very different for you. In fact, I would be surprised if it wasn't, for I think we all experience these entities in our own unique ways. Some people perceive them on a more emotional or intuitive level, while others, like myself, find them more analytical in nature. The point is, as you practice this discipline, you will eventually grow to "know" the entity, making it easier to recognize when it is and isn't there, thereby reducing the chances that you will be fooled.

How the Guide Works

Obviously, a guide is going to work in different ways depending upon one's personality, needs, and level of spiritual maturity. As such, I can only speak to my own experiences and make no specific claims in regard to them, but recount them now only in the hope the reader will find them both interesting and potentially instructive. Additionally, they are typical only for myself; any such interactions or experiences you might have will undoubtedly be very different in nature, and so you would be wise to approach the rest of this chapter with that in mind.

First of all, I have discovered that seeking advice from one's spirit guide should not be a substitute for analytical and rational thinking but should instead be seen as an aid to it. It seems to work by helping you better understand the options available before you and permitting you to see all the ramifications of each decision. In other words, a guide's advice is designed to bring us clarity, sharpen our focus, and help us build upon the wisdom that already resides within us. In effect, it recognizes that the answers lie within ourselves and simply steers us in that direction.

Some might consider this just another term for concentrating (something which is obviously quite possible to do outside a spiritual venue), and I do not deny that. Anyone can concentrate on a problem and think it through without having to call upon the help of a spirit guide. However, there is a difference in that it is my experience that when I focus in on these energies and seek their guidance, I perceive possibilities that I did not see when I tried to think them through independent of "outside" help. I suppose some would consider this just an illusion on my part, but all I know is that I see a difference when I ponder a problem on my own and when I bring the universal consciousness into the mix.

It's not the difference between night and day, but more akin to the difference between a cloudy day and a sunny one.

This book is a good example of what I'm talking about and how my guide works in my life. When I first sat down to put it together, I had only a vague notion of how I wanted the information ordered and what sort of material I wanted to include in it. However, as I began working on it, a strange thing happened. Ideas suddenly occurred to me that I hadn't considered before. Chapters seemed to practically write themselves. Whole sections started to come together, while ideas that I was having trouble fleshing out suddenly became clear to me. I could leave a chapter in mid-thought and come back to it a week later and pick up precisely where I had left off. It didn't always run smoothly, of course, but over the months it has taken me to develop this manuscript, I have been astonished at how effortlessly it has gone together—almost as if it is being "guided" in some way. I'm not maintaining that this book was channeled or that I received direct information from supernatural entities; I do, however, believe that as I was able to tap into the energies of my "spirit guide" and listen to it, the work became easier and the book began to flow better.

By way of a further example, this entire chapter on spirit guides was never a part of my original manuscript, but emerged spontaneously out of the earlier chapter on spirit communication (which itself was a later addendum to my original body of work). I recall working on that chapter and when I got to the section on spirit guides, I suddenly felt compelled to expand it into an entirely new chapter. Unfortunately, I only had about two thousand words in that section—hardly enough for an entire chapter—but as I began following my instincts, it blossomed into more than enough for a full chapter as new ideas and perceptions came to me. Of course, I still had to do the "heavy lifting," but the process by which they got here seemed to be directed, as though there was "someone" leaning over my shoulder giving me suggestions while I worked.

That, I think, is the best illustration of how a spirit guide works; it doesn't do the work for you—it just assists you in making the work flow more smoothly. At least, that is how my guide seems to work for me. Yours will undoubtedly use a very different tack, one perfectly fashioned to meet your needs and make the best use of your energies, skills, and talents, which is exactly the way it should be.

Conclusion

The idea that there may be higher powers that are willing and able to help us in our own spiritual and social progress should be no more remarkable or difficult to accept than should the idea that God exists or that human consciousness might survive death. After all, in a way they are all just different elements of the same thing, and, since all of them lie outside the realm of empirical science's ability to either prove or disprove, that leaves plenty of room for things like spirit guides to exist.

Further, the idea that the universe is made up of an infinite variety of beings should not only be credible, but even expected. Unless one insists on maintaining a purely naturalistic/materialist view of reality that rejects all notions of the supernatural, the paranormal, or the divine, we should be willing to accept the possibility that there is a great deal more going on in the universe, as well as within our world, than we can begin to fathom. The idea that spirit guides exist and that we may communicate with them has to be considered a reasonable part of the mix; to refuse to do so is to question the very premise that we, along with all of life, are a unified part of a greater whole and that each part of that greater whole is passionately interested in what happens to the other parts. In essence, I believe the entire universe has a stake in our spiritual evolution and, as such, is willing and, indeed, even compelled to get involved in helping that process along.

However, it will only help us as much as we are willing to let it, for the universe will never override our primary right to self-determination and free will, even if those things ultimately result in hardship and great difficulties. It is an unflinchingly level playing surface we have before us, one that permits us and others to experience both the blessing—and the consequences—of the decisions we make, regardless of how they may affect us. This should demonstrate better than anything else that we truly live in a unique and wonderful universe, the knowledge of which is perhaps the greatest gift of all.

Conclusion

It is an unavoidable reality that it may never be possible to prove the existence of ghosts with anything approaching scientific certainty. Such evidence, I suspect, will always, for a variety of reasons, remain just outside our reach, tantalizing us with its seemingly substantive nature but never quite managing to finally "deliver the goods."

But is that necessarily a bad thing?

Consider what it would mean if we could prove empirically that consciousness and/or personality does survive the death of the body. What moral, economic, political, and spiritual repercussions might that have? For example, could a disembodied personality retain ownership rights over the property it once resided at and is currently haunting and, if so, would a prospective buyer have to get the permission of the haunting entity before a sale could be finalized? Could the testimony of a spiritual entity be entered into evidence in a murder trial? And if not, why not? And consider the potential profit, and the catastrophic consequences, if one were ever able to develop a mechanism by which we might easily converse with those who have passed over with no more difficulty than we experience today in using a cell phone?[51]

And this, of course, doesn't even begin to scratch the surface of how such a reality would affect society, our culture, and even religion

---

51. Inventor Thomas Edison was, in fact, working on just such a device shortly before his death in 1931.

itself. Would all the world's great faiths have to be abandoned or would they instead merge into a single belief system in which mediums and psychics of all persuasions and ethics were its high priests and priestesses? And what profound changes might be wrought within those nations where traditional religious beliefs serve as the basic foundation of their society? Could it be enough to precipitate the greatest social and moral upheaval in human history and dramatically reshape our modern culture in unique and unpredictable ways? No, it is better that ghosts never be proven to the satisfaction of science, for I suspect the merging of the physical and spiritual realms would be too traumatic for either to survive intact.

These realms of existence are separate for a very good reason. The physical realm is the "proving grounds" of the soul; the place where pure intellect and disembodied consciousness can manifest so as to sharpen its spiritual edge and experience life from a multitude of perspectives. For it to be an effective means of spiritual development, however, it must remain apart from and even, to some degree, largely ignorant of the realm from whence it came lest the entire game be compromised. In the same way that even the best flight simulator can never capture the true exhilaration of aerial combat as long as the student knows it is only an illusion, knowing too much about what is really going on from the perspective of eternity diminishes the experience of living in the here and now. After all, even the best re-creations are of value only if the person undergoing them remains ignorant of the fact that he or she is only witnessing an illusion. In the same way then, it is equally as important that we remain ignorant of the spiritual realm if we are to genuinely experience anything here in the physical realm.

That, however, does not mean we can't still have some fun exploring the issue, for the universe is really a great, playful theater that is okay with the idea of giving the curious a peek behind the curtain to observe some of the backstage workings. In many ways, it is like a skilled magician who is willing to demonstrate how a trick works but only to those who are respectful of the magician's craft and, of course, with the understanding that learning too much can spoil the illusion, which is the reason only those intent on truly understanding the spiritual realm need apply.

Beyond the profound moral and scientific repercussions that the possible existence of ghosts entails, however, I hope this book has demonstrated nothing so much as that ghosts are not something that exists apart from ourselves, but that they are and have always been a part of us, for they are nothing more (or less) than our fellow human beings experiencing existence from within another context. In that they are also beings still apparently capable of great love and compassion, however, they give all of us reason to hope as well, for they demonstrate that the great human denominator of love not only transcends our own mortality, but that in the end, it may be all that truly exists in the universe. If that doesn't give people reason to be optimistic, I can't imagine what might do it.

In the end, we cannot escape the fact that ghosts have been and remain a part of the human experience. They may be at times mischievous, frightening, menacing, or even dangerous (though no more so than are our still living colleagues), but throughout it all they have stubbornly managed to remain a part of every culture around the world since mankind first began to tell stories around the communal campfire. They have been recorded in the ancient writings of the Romans and Greeks, and have even found mention in the Bible. They transcend time and culture like few phenomena can, and maintain a startling degree of consistency far beyond that which can be found in the near universal belief in God.

But are they all simply a means by which we mere mortals try to deal with our own inevitable demise, or are they genuinely external phenomena that we are only just beginning to understand? I suppose the answer to that depends upon one's worldview and understanding of reality. To the strict materialist they do not exist because once we are dead, *we* do not exist. To many theists, ghosts do not exist because to die means to be instantly transported to another realm of existence—either heaven or hell—with no intermediate stops in between. But to those who are not so blessed with such postmortem certainty or are at least willing to recognize their own substantial limitations in terms of understanding the universe, they remain a very real possibility.

In the end it is up to us to decide what this phenomena has to say to us, which is perhaps its greatest value. It forces us to take a position about our own mortality and let that position influence our beliefs, our behaviors, and our plans for the future. It is important not so much for what it tells us about the possibility of an afterlife, but for what it tells us about ourselves in the here and now, for ghosts, regardless of how one wishes to define or explain them away, are an important tool in our own spiritual growth and awareness. Such an idea should give all of us cause to appreciate the intricate and perfect beauty of the universe within which we all experience our own unique reality.

> *Scrooge fell upon his knees, and clasped his hands before his face. "Mercy!" he said. "Dreadful apparition, why do you trouble me?"*
>
> *"Man of the worldly mind!" replied the Ghost, "do you believe in me or not?"*
>
> *"I do," said Scrooge. "I must. But why do spirits walk the earth, and why do they come to me?"*
>
> *"It is required of every man," the Ghost returned, "that the spirit within him should walk abroad among his fellow-men, and travel far and wide; and if that spirit goes not forth in life, it is condemned to do so after death. It is doomed to wander through the world—oh, woe is me!—and witness what it cannot share, but might have shared on earth, and turned to happiness."*
>
> —Charles Dickens, *A Christmas Carol*

Bibliography

Auerbach, Loyd. *Ghost Hunting: How to Investigate the Paranormal.* Oakland: Ronin Publishing, 2004.

Chambers, Dr. Paul. *Sex and the Paranormal.* UK: Blandford Pr., 1999.

Fuller, John G. *The Ghost of Flight 401.* Berkley Publishing Group, 1976.

Holzer, Hanz. *Ghosts: True Encounters with the World Beyond.* Black Dog & Leventhal Publishers, 1997.

———— *Life Beyond: Compelling Evidence for Past Lives & Existence After Death.* McGraw-Hill, 1994.

Morris, Mark Alan. *The Ghost Next Door.* iUniverse Star, 2004.

Steiger, Brad. *Real Ghosts, Restless Spirits & Haunted Places.* Visible Ink Press, 2003.

Taylor, Troy. *Ghost Hunter's Guidebook.* Whitechapel Productions, 2001.

USA Weekend. *I Never Believed in Ghosts Until . . .* McGraw-Hill, 1992.

Warren, Joshua. *How To Hunt Ghosts.* Simon & Schuster, 2003.

Wilson, Colin. *Afterlife.* London: Harrap Lmtd., 1985.

———— *Beyond the Occult.* New York: Carroll & Graf Publishers, 1989.

"Channeled" or "Inspired" Books

Roberts, Jane. *Seth Speaks.* Bantam, 1966.

Schucman, Helen. *A Course in Miracles.* Foundation for Inner Peace, 1975.

Walsch, Neale Donald. *Conversations with God, Book 1.* G.P. Putnam's Sons, 1995.

———— *Conversations with God, Book 2.* Hampton Roads, 1997.

———— *Conversations with God, Book 3.* Hampton Roads, 1998.

Books Dealing Primarily with Reincarnation

Danelek, J. Allan. *Mystery of Reincarnation.* St. Paul, MN: Llewellyn Publications, 2005.

Newton, Dr. Michael. *Journey of Souls: Case Studies of Life Between Lives.* St. Paul, MN: Llewellyn Publications, 1994.

Stevenson, Dr. Ian. *Twenty Cases Suggestive of Reincarnation.* American Society for Psychical Research, 1966.

Wambach, Dr. Helen. *Reliving Past Lives.* Barnes & Noble, Inc., 1978.

Weiss, Dr. Brian. *Many Lives, Many Masters.* Simon & Schuster, 1988.